no easy answers

the truth behind death at columbine

What People Are Saying About
no easy answers

"Brown's discussion of Harris's Web pages, where he made a death threat against Brown, and the police's failure to act on them, makes for chilling reading....[R]eaders interested in a close-up account of the tragedy will want to read this book."

—Publishers Weekly

"Brown's story is gripping and provocative....Excellent choice for outsider teens wondering if there's a light at the end of the bullying tunnel."

—Booklist

"[The book] gives a perspective no one else could...It shows a side you cannot get anywhere else."

—Brian Rohrbough, father of Columbine victim Daniel Rohrbough

no easy answers

the truth behind death at columbine

brooks brown and rob merritt

Lantern Books ● New York
A Division of Booklight Inc.

2002
Lantern Books
One Union Square West, Suite 201
New York, NY 10003

Notice

Brooks Brown was involved in and has personal knowledge of many aspects of the events described in this book. In some instances quotations of conversations in this text are his best recollections of conversations had by or with him, or overheard by him, and may not be verbatim; in other instances quotes are reasonable interpretations of what was said or likely to have been said, consistent with the author's experience of the situation and people involved.

Rights to the trademarks, product names, or any derivatives of such trademarks or names are neither claimed, intended, nor implied by the author or publisher of this work.

All efforts have been made to locate and obtain permission from the owners of the photographic images used in this book.

Library of Congress Cataloging-in-Publication Data

Brown, Brooks.
   No easy answers : the truth behind death at Columbine High School / by Brooks Brown and Rob Merritt.
      p. cm.
   ISBN 1-59056-031-0 (alk. paper)
1. School shootings—Colorado—Littleton. 2. Teenagers—United States—Social conditions—20th century—Case studies. 3. Brown, Brooks. 4. Columbine High School (Littleton, Colo.)—Students—Biography. I. Merritt, Rob, 1976- II. Title.
   LB3013.33.C6 B76 2002
   373.788'82—dc21

                                                                      2002010415

Acknowledgments

BROOKS BROWN
Thanks to:

ROB MERRITT FOR UNDERTAKING SUCH A DIFFICULT TASK WITH ME
and helping me through it. Meagan Fishell for sticking by me through all
the shit I've gone through. Michael Troutman, Trevor Dolac, Scott
Parker, Brendt Scholle, Adam Calhoun, Derek, Jaysen, Jaymz, Ninja,
Injun, and Jamin for being the friends you are. My parents, Randy and
Judy, for instilling in me early on the ability to endure and care, and for
sticking by me when I am most lost. My brother, Aaron, for giving me
ways to have fun over the last three years. My cousin Josh for giving me
someone to talk to.

Michael Moore and his entire staff, especially Rehya, for believing in
me without having to ask the standard questions. Anne Sullivan at
Lantern Books for proving the importance of never giving up. Spike and
Brad Xavier, Lou Dog, Bobby B, D-Loc, Richter, Insane Clown Posse,
Twizted, anybody killer, Taxman, Pak, and The Wind for proving that
people can make good music and not be sellouts.

Troy Manuello, Eric Kritzer, Jan Jankowski, Susan Caruthers, and
the janitors of Columbine High School. You were all that kept me in that
school, let alone taught me how to enjoy learning and enjoy people.

And thanks to anyone I missed. My Juggalos, family, people who mean a lot to me, everyone. I owe a lotta people for getting through the last few years. You should know who you are.

ROB MERRITT
Thanks to:

BROOKS BROWN FOR TRUSTING ME ENOUGH TO BRING ME ON board for such a personal project; Eddie Morris, Andy Paugh, and Jenny Welp for their critical feedback on early drafts; Randy, Judy, and Aaron Brown for their assistance at every step of the way; Brian Rohrbough and Richard Castaldo, not only for helping me understand their losses, but for their refusal to give up in the face of them; Anne Sullivan at Lantern Books, who championed our project from the beginning; Sarah Gallogly at Lantern for her invaluable guidance; and my parents, Richard and Linda Merritt, for their love and encouragement.

Also, thanks to Pat Dunleavy, David Horton, Ron Smrha, Robert Geuder, Michael J. Peitz, and John and Diane Rosteck for proving that when teachers make the extra effort to touch a student's life and inspire him, it can make all the difference.

Finally, special thanks go to Jamie Christenson, the most amazing friend and inspiration I ever could have asked for. She loved this project and supported it with everything she had, but she did not live to see its publication. I love her with all my heart. This book is for her.

Contents

Part One: Columbine

Part Two: Aftermath

Part One

COLUMBINE

1

"get out of here"

THE LAST TIME I STOOD IN THIS SPOT, THE WORLD AS I KNEW IT WAS about to be shattered.

I'm alone on a staircase outside Columbine High School in Littleton, Colorado. The spot is a quiet one, bordered by concrete recesses that merge into a sidewalk leading up toward the math wing. I've stood here many times before; this place was always secluded enough for me to get in one last quick drag before an administrator would yell at me to quit smoking on school grounds.

Today it's far away from the pool of media trucks gathered nearby in Clement Park, and from the gymnasium where the big assembly of students and teachers is taking place. It's a good place for me to just stop and think.

It's also a good place to mourn.

I haven't stood here since April 20, 1999. I haven't stood here since exactly one year ago this minute.

For the first two periods of April 20, it had been a typical day at Columbine, no different from any other in the past four years. Finished first hour, went outside, had a cigarette. Went to second hour, where I worked as an assistant to Mrs. Caruthers, the theatre teacher. She handed me some papers to help her review and grade. When the period ended, I went out and had a cigarette.

Looking around during that smoke break, I realized what a beautiful day it was, especially for April, when in Colorado we're used to rain. The sun was out, the sky was clear and blue, and temperatures were finally warming up after the past few months of winter. I was wearing a white T-shirt and jeans; I hadn't even bothered bringing a coat to school.

I finished my cigarette and headed for philosophy class. We had a test that day on Chinese philosophy. I was never a great student at Columbine, but I felt all right about this particular test. Mr. Kritzer was the kind of teacher who truly understood the material he taught—and knew that allowing students to contribute their own ideas, without being judgmental, is critical in the teaching of philosophy. His approach made me enjoy the class, which in turn made me work harder. I had a good feeling about today.

That was when I noticed something odd. Eric wasn't there.

It didn't seem right. My friend Eric Harris skipped class all the time, but he knew this wasn't just a quiz we were taking that morning. The test was going to be worth a good third of our final grade. To miss it was basically to write off the rest of the term.

I tried to shrug it off as his loss. Still, I was a little concerned. Eric was a good student, and his parents drove him hard when it came to grades. I knew I'd have to give him shit about it the next time I saw him.

I finished my test and brought it up to the front of the room. The period ended, and off I went to have another cigarette. Then I headed to fourth-hour creative writing.

Once again, no Eric. This time, no Dylan, either.

Normally, this wouldn't have seemed that odd. Eric was best friends with Dylan Klebold, and the two of them ditched creative writing all the time. However, they usually had at least one of their other friends from this class with them, too. Today, though, Becca Heins, Nate Dykeman, and I had all showed up for class. Apparently none of us had been invited along.

I don't really remember what Mrs. Kelly had us do that day. I was already thinking about going home after fourth period and missing my last class. I had stayed up late on my computer the night before, and I was tired. I already had my cigarettes in hand by the time the bell rang to signify the end of the period.

I had no idea that this would be the last time I would ever attend a class at Columbine High School. That it was the last time I'd ever take a philosophy test, or write a paper for Mrs. Kelly, or grade papers for Mrs. Caruthers, or play dodgeball in gym class.

The world I knew was about to be altered forever.

As I took a drag on my cigarette, I was a little surprised to see Eric suddenly pull into the parking lot right in front of me. It seemed strange that he would skip two classes, then suddenly show up back at school.

Even more bizarre, he was pulling into a spot other than his assigned space.

I wanted to talk with him. I still couldn't believe he'd skipped philosophy. I walked right up to his car, just as he was getting out, and with a mix of concern and friendly cruelty, I started cussing him out.

"What the hell's wrong with you, man?" I said. "You weren't in third hour today. You missed the test!"

I didn't know how to read the look he gave me. It wasn't the "Oh, damn" look of someone who had just realized what was about to happen to his grades, or the look of annoyance that your friends give you when you rib them about a screw-up. This was something very different.

He laughed at me, as if he couldn't believe I had even brought the subject up. "It doesn't matter anymore," he said. He pulled a light blue gym bag out of the backseat and set it down on the ground.

"Yeah, whatever," I muttered, taking another drag on my cigarette. Eric was a weird guy—cool, but not as good a friend as Dylan. But today he was acting a little stranger than usual.

Eric stopped. He looked straight at me.

"Brooks, I like you now," he said. "Get out of here. Go home."

His tone was bizarre—intense, but almost chuckling. I'd never heard him talk that way before.

That's when I noticed Eric wasn't wearing his hat. A pretty small detail, I suppose; he was wearing his usual attire of black pants and a white T-shirt, so everything else seemed normal. But Eric always wore his hat. Always.

Eric didn't even hold my gaze after he spoke. He turned his back to me and started pulling another duffel bag out of his back seat.

"Uh, okay, whatever," I said.

Eric didn't say anything else. He wasn't even looking at me anymore. My presence didn't seem to mean anything to him now.

I took another drag off my cigarette—and that's when I got hit by this uneasy feeling. Didn't know where it came from, but somehow, in the back of my mind, I knew something wasn't right. The hat. Eric's demeanor. The test he'd skipped. I couldn't pin down why alarms are going off in my head. But they were. Something was telling me that I needed to walk away.

Eric was a very serious person. You didn't screw with him. I knew that from last year, when he'd posted messages on the Internet about how badly he wanted me dead. We had made peace afterwards; I thought all of that was behind us now. But maybe those memories were coming back to unsettle me all over again.

Whatever the reason, somehow I knew that Eric was not one to be antagonized any further at this moment.

I didn't say anything else. I walked across the parking lot back down to Pierce Street, still holding the same cigarette I had lit when I walked out of class. I tried to just keep smoking like nothing had happened. Yet deep down, I knew that something was wrong, and that it had to do with Eric.

Was he going to play a prank? Mess with the school's ventilation system? Shoot paint balls? Set off a pipe bomb in the parking lot?

I saw an image of Bart Simpson flushing a lit firecracker down the toilet right before Principal Skinner brings his mother in to use the facilities. It had always made me laugh in the past. For some reason it didn't now.

I finished the cigarette and tossed it. I tried to forget about Eric for a moment and decide whether I was going to skip fifth hour or not.

Then I heard a loud crack in the distance.

I looked around. Funny, I thought, that almost sounded like a gunshot. I looked to my left. On the other side of Pierce, there was a whole block of housing construction going on. Had I just heard a nail gun? Maybe. The pounding of nails will echo everywhere. You can't pinpoint where it came from when it's that loud.

I heard a few more cracks. They sounded different from nails. Couldn't be sure. Then I heard something much louder than what had come before.

That wasn't any goddamn nail.

In that instant, I knew something horrible was happening. Panic washed over me, and without even thinking about it, I started moving. I didn't know what was going on, but somehow I knew I had to get as far away from there as possible.

I heard more loud cracks. Something that sounded like explosions. A bomb. I wasn't walking anymore. I was running on Pierce Street, wanting in that instant to get as far away from Columbine as possible.

One block. Another. Loud noises coming from behind me, sounds I knew meant unimaginable horror.

I reached a little green generator next to the sidewalk and sat down for a moment. I could just barely see the front edge of Columbine, at the top of the hill in the distance, and I could still hear the shots.

"All right—gotta figure out what I'm doing—gotta figure out what I'm doing—"

I had no idea what I was going to do.

I tried to calm myself down. Maybe it's a prank, I thought. Maybe it's exactly what I thought before. Maybe Eric tossed a couple of pipe bombs, scared the teachers, and now he's hiding behind a few cars in the parking lot, laughing his ass off.

If it was a prank, and I ran to someone's house and started screaming that there were bombs and explosions going off at Columbine, what would be the first thing they'd do? Call the cops. If I was wrong, what would happen then? I'd get slapped with a fine. Nailed. You get in trouble real bad for making false reports in Littleton.

Besides, I thought, maybe I didn't hear anything. Maybe I'm just losing it. Maybe if I just get up and walk back, I'll see that nothing happened and everything's all right.

Jesus. I didn't know what the hell to think.

But I couldn't stay there on that generator, out in the open. I knew that.

I got up and kept moving away from the school. I was three blocks away from Columbine when I reached a concrete bicycle underpass that goes right under Pierce Street. I jumped down off the sidewalk and disappeared into it.

I'd gone down here to smoke with friends in the past. I'd never done it to try to protect myself.

My hands were shaking as I pulled out another cigarette. I had to clear my mind.

I replayed everything from the past ten minutes. The explosions. The shotgun blast. It had to be a shotgun blast. Had to be, had to be ... I thought back to my conversation with Eric. Had I missed something? A detail, something sticking out of his bag? Anything?

And then it hit me—the sick realization.

Eric.

Son of a bitch.

I suddenly remembered all the articles I'd read about Jonesboro and Pearl and Paducah, and Kip Kinkel and Michael Carneal and Luke Woodham. I remembered those times when we'd laughed in speech class that Columbine was next. We'd said that if any school was ripe to get shot up, it was ours.

Now it was happening, and my friend was behind it.

Oh, man. No. No. Jesus, Eric, what the hell are you doing?

Christ, I thought. *Get it together. Come on. What if I'm the only one who knows? What if the cops don't have a name? I've got to find a phone. I have to get out of here.*

I heard police cars driving overhead as I hurried back out from the underpass. I looked out across the empty lots, to where the closest house was, several hundred yards away.

Then I heard it. I turned around just in time to see a massive barrage of police cruisers, a dozen of them if not more, thundering north on Pierce toward the school with sirens wailing. If I needed any further confirmation that this was real, I found it when I saw half the police force of Jefferson County descending on Columbine.

I ran to the first house I saw and started hammering on the door. Nothing. I ran for the next one and did the same thing. I don't know if I was yelling through the door or not. It didn't seem to matter.

As I ran to the next one, I saw a woman getting into her car with her daughter. She looked like she was rushing.

"I need your phone!" I yelled to her. "Please let me use your phone!"

"No, no," she said, hurrying into her car. "I have to leave."

With that, she barreled out of there. I think I scared her.

As she left, I saw two other women outside the house. One of them was Mrs. Taylor; I knew her daughter Anna, a very sweet girl who had been in several classes with me over the years. Her mother recognized me—and saw the look on my face.

"What's wrong?" she asked.

"I need to use your phone." I was breathing hard, sweating, scared out of my mind. She asked me why.

I said I didn't want to freak her out, but that I thought there had been a shooting at Columbine.

Mrs. Taylor stayed calm. "Okay," she said. "You lie down. Lie on your back. I'll go get the phone. You just try to relax for a second."

I sat down, burying my head in my lap. Then I lay back with my arm over my face, trying to regain my composure. I still didn't know for sure what was happening. I still felt panicked.

Mrs. Taylor gave me the phone. I called my dad at work.

"Have you heard anything on the news?" I said.

"No," he replied. "Why? Brooks, what's going on?"

"Well, first of all, I want you to know that I'm all right. I'm out of the school and I'm fine."

"Okay ..."

"Dad, I think Eric's shooting up Columbine."

There was a pause on the other end. "What?!"

"Dad, something's going on," I continued. "I don't know what to do."

"I'll be there in ten minutes! Where do you want me to meet you?"

I looked down the street, trying to place my own location.

"I'll meet you by Steve's house on Upham Street. I'm right by there." Steve was my drum teacher, so my dad knew where he lived.

"Okay. Ten minutes, Brooks. Thanks."

My dad hung up and I handed the phone back to Mrs. Taylor. I thanked her, and apologized if I had panicked her. I knew her daughter was in choir right now.

That was when I realized. *My brother's still in there.*

My little brother Aaron, two grades below me, was also a student at Columbine. He and Eric didn't get along. If Eric was still in the school, and he came across my brother ... I felt terror overwhelming me all over again.

I started walking toward Steve's house. A lot of cars were already driving by; the first thing I did was look among them for people I knew.

First I saw Mr. Johnson and Mr. Bath, two of my teachers from Columbine, and waved them down. They pulled over and asked me why I wasn't in class. They were laughing.

I just blurted out what I thought: Eric Harris was involved in a shooting of some kind. They both became very quiet.

"You know, he's in my psychology class," Mr. Johnson said after a beat.

Mr. Bath asked if I was okay. I told them yeah, and they said they would see me later. Then they drove off. I kept walking, until my friend Ryan Schwayder drove up in his Jeep Grand Cherokee.

"Hey, Brooks," he said. "What's going on? We tried to go back to school and they've got the road blocked off."

I didn't answer him. I just opened the door, threw my book bag into the back of the Jeep and jumped in. Inside were two other Columbine students, Matt Houck and Deanna Shaffer.

Ryan took one look at me and instantly became concerned. "What's wrong?"

I tried to explain, but I was talking too fast for them to understand. Ryan kept asking me to slow down. I took a couple of deep breaths, and asked Ryan to drive closer to Columbine, so I could get a better look.

"Why? What's wrong?"

I took a moment. "There's a shooting at the school."

For two seconds, dead silence filled the Jeep.

Then Deanna's hands went to her face, and she started crying. Ryan's entire body just sank in his seat; I could literally see the energy escape him.

"Oh, God," Matt said quietly.

I tried to explain about seeing Eric, and what he had said to me. "Oh, man, I think he had a duffel bag with him," I said.

I asked Ryan if I could use his phone to call 911. Almost like a zombie, he handed it to me. I called the police and told them I had information about what was happening.

They seemed to have trouble transferring my call at first. I wound up getting forwarded to the Arapahoe County office. As this was happening, all of us looked up to see multiple helicopters descending on our school.

The battery started dying on Ryan's phone. He let me climb over into the driver's seat and plug the phone into the lighter adapter to get power, while he stood outside with Deanna, quietly holding her.

Arapahoe County put me through to Detective Kirby Hodgkin, and I started rattling off information. I told them about Eric skipping class that day, what he'd said to me in the parking lot, what kind of car he drove, and what he was wearing.

"He looked like an Army cadet," I said.

I said Eric had just turned eighteen a few weeks ago, and that he'd talked in class about buying guns, saying he "couldn't wait to turn eighteen" so he could legally purchase one. I mentioned that we'd had a falling-out several years before. I didn't think to mention the Web pages.

While I was still on the phone with them, my dad pulled up next to us. "We're getting the hell out of here right now!" he yelled.

I didn't know what had my dad so spooked. He later told me that he'd heard a report on the radio saying the shooters had already left the school on foot. My dad was afraid that Eric was walking around in the same neighborhood as us. With guns.

I said, "Fine! Fine!" I didn't even take time to change places with Ryan. He and Deanna jumped back in the car, and with me behind the wheel, we took off behind my dad.

We headed back out to Pierce Street and floored it the rest of the way to our house, not caring that we were probably pushing sixty, sixty-five miles per hour on residential streets. I was still on the phone, so I explained the situation to the detective at Arapahoe County. He took my address and said that an officer would come out later that day to interview me further.

My dad and I tore around the last few corners leading to our house. He pulled up on the sidewalk, and I parked right behind him—just as my brother Aaron came running out of the house to meet us.

Thank God, I thought. I was so happy to see him safe.

When my dad came to get me, he already knew Aaron was okay. After he'd talked to me, Aaron had called to let him know he had made it home. My dad knew I was the only kid he still had to bring to safety.

Aaron told me that he and his friends had run like hell to get out of the school, made it to his car, and then come home. He didn't tell me how he'd been sitting in the cafeteria when it started, just a few tables away from a propane bomb that had somehow failed to detonate. Or how he'd run through the auditorium, being chased by the gunmen, bullets flying over his head, hearing the girl behind him get hit and scream, "I'm shot!" I would learn about that much later.

All we knew was that we were safe at home. Far away from the horror that was still unfolding at Columbine High School.

"Brooks, I like you now. Get out of here. Go home."

Those wound up being Eric Harris's last words to me.

Five minutes after I spoke to him, he was hurling pipe bombs at my friends, firing shotgun blasts at my brother, and murdering innocent students—students whose biggest worries before that moment had been midterm tests and college applications.

Yet what I didn't know at the time was that Eric wasn't alone in his mission. His best friend Dylan Klebold was with him, firing off bullets right next to him, hunting and killing—and laughing about it.

Dylan. One of my closest friends since first grade.

Soon, Eric and Dylan would kill themselves in the library, denying any of us the chance to question them. I'd never be able to sit down across from the guy I used to throw snowballs at in elementary school and ask him why he had wanted to kill all those people who had done him no wrong whatsoever.

The hell that Eric and Dylan would create at my high school that day would go on to haunt their families, the families of the victims, and parents and students throughout our community and the world. It would destroy my life, as comments from the sheriff would lead to accusations that I was somehow involved in the plot.

Worst of all, it left me struggling with the knowledge that not only were my classmates dead, they had been murdered by one friend I'd known since childhood—and another who had let me walk away only a few minutes beforehand. And I would never be able to ask them why.

So today I'm standing at that same spot where I watched as the end of my world came driving into Columbine's parking lot. I'm standing alone, smoking a cigarette, the same way I did then. Thinking. Reflecting. Trying to make sense of everything.

Inside the school, our principal, Frank DeAngelis, is leading a collection of students and staff in a massive spirit assembly, reading aloud the words of President Clinton, telling everyone that we're all going to move forward, that the hate in our world "must turn to love."

At least, that's what I would read in the papers later. I didn't see it. I didn't hear it. I wasn't interested—nor did I have much of an interest in the "closure stories" being prepared by the pool of media nearby in Clement Park, ready to close the door on Columbine and declare the whole thing as the work of two sick, deranged kids who represent nothing more than the work of the devil, or of violent video games, or just aberrations in an otherwise perfectly civilized high school.

I knew how ludicrous that was. I knew that we were nowhere near closure on Columbine. We still aren't. I knew Eric and Dylan far better than these analysts who were telling us about the harmful effects of *Doom*. I knew them far better than Principal DeAngelis, who behind his tears and speeches had no time for the kids like us, who existed outside the norm and were punished daily by our peers because of it.

I knew that there were more Erics and Dylans out there, and I knew why their disenchantment was growing. I could see the void they were falling into—and I knew that void was getting bigger.

So I'm mourning the dead today, standing in this spot—this spot that never used to be anything significant—for the first time in a year. But I'm not interested in praying for a solution. I'm interested in finding one right now, in the real world.

This book is my first step.

2

why?

FROM THE MOMENT I CHOSE TO BEGIN THIS PROJECT, I KNEW THERE would be people criticizing me for it. Many people think that "Columbine is done"—that it's something not worth dredging up again, because we've heard enough about what happened. "It's time to move on," they say.

The reason they say this is that the public has settled on what they think caused Columbine: two sick, crazy boys who killed people because they were completely different from the rest of us. "It's a tragic thing," they'll say, "but not something that requires any further thought." There are some who still question the behavior of the police that day—as well they should—but there aren't many who are still asking questions about the killers themselves.

Except, of course, for young people.

The people who are still in high school know what's going on. They know there's something much, much bigger behind Columbine than what the rest of the world has been led to believe. These folks want to know who Eric and Dylan were. They want to know why two kids who are just like the people they share the school hallways with every day would turn around and do what they did.

Why? Because they see parallels with Columbine at their own schools every day.

The kids asking these questions are the kids who play video games like *Doom*, but don't feel the urge to imitate them in real life. They're the juggalos who listen to Insane Clown Posse rap about brutality and serial killers, but have no desire to kill anyone. They're the "loner" kids who have exhibited all the "warning signs" that experts go on the talk shows about, yet are still doing fine.

These are the kids who hear politicians blaming TV and music and video games, and shake their heads, because they know that's not where the problem really lies. These are the kids who can feel the pull of something else out there—the real cause of Eric and Dylan—and are asking themselves what it is.

Many people aren't willing to get their hands dirty by probing the true reasons behind what happened at Columbine. It's easier to believe in quick fixes than to accept what the real problems might be.

After all, what's the easier sell for a politician: to go out there and tell people that they've screwed up, that they need to take better care of their kids, that they've created an ugly, uncaring society for the next generation, and that we need to search our own souls for a solution?

Or to just tell them that the evil entertainment industry is ruining our kids?

It's the second option that many seem to prefer. It gets big ratings on TV and high approval ratings for politicians, and makes everybody feel good by providing them with a designated villain. It's much easier to say that *Doom* and *South Park* are ruining our children than to think that maybe we have something to do with it, too.

Want to blame the entertainment industry? Consider this: The entertainment industry makes money by giving people what they want. The day that violent movies stop turning a profit, violent movies will disappear. The day that fighting games lose their appeal is the day that games like *Mortal Kombat* will vanish. The day that teenagers no longer relate to the angry music of Limp Bizkit or Nine Inch Nails is the day those bands will cease to sell records. The entertainment industry doesn't impose some kind of evil personality on consumers that's foreign to us; it feeds on who we are and how we live.

Even so, the music industry was one of the biggest targets criticized after the attack on Columbine. Eric and Dylan were huge fans of German techno/metal. They were especially partial to bands like Rammstein and KMFDM; since Eric had taken German for years, he could translate the lyrics, and he liked the fact that others couldn't understand what he was listening to. Eric put quotes from his favorite bands on his Web site. He wore a KMFDM hat to school all the time. His co-workers at Blackjack Pizza say he was always singing the praises of his favorite bands and trying to get others to listen to them.

After Columbine happened, Rammstein and KMFDM became "villains" in the eyes of the pro-censorship folk. TV news reports pulled out one quote from Rammstein that went, "You in the schoolyard / I'm ready for killing."

Yet music doesn't teach people to kill. Music creates an emotion, whether it's anger, sorrow, thoughtfulness, happiness, or humor. What people do with their emotions is up to them. But music doesn't tell people what to do.

Some have criticized Insane Clown Posse because their lyrics involve sex, murder, and brutality, laced with dark humor. But ICP themselves put it best: they're wearing clown makeup. If you take what they have to say that seriously, then you have something wrong with you—and that's not ICP's fault.

Marilyn Manson wears a $25 white contact lens in his left eye. He wears costumes onstage. These are not the sages of our age. They aren't leaders. They are entertainers. And although Marilyn Manson, ICP, and

Rammstein have some songs with a very powerful message, they aren't trying to change the world. They're just writing about what they think.

So why is their music so violent? Simple—our society is a violent culture in and of itself, and our music is a reflection of that.

Ayn Rand wrote, "Would you follow the advice of someone who told you that you must fight tuberculosis by confining the treatment to its symptoms—that you must treat the cough, the high temperature, the loss of weight—but must refuse to consider or to touch its cause, the germs in the patient's lungs, in order not to antagonize the germs? Do not adopt such a course in politics."

Music is the same way; it's a symptom, not a cause. Violent music did not just appear one day and unleash violence upon the world. Society created violent music, because there was something happening in society that made that kind of music appealing.

So the bigger question is this: What is happening to make society want this kind of entertainment? What do kids see happening in real life that makes violent video games so appealing?

Every day on the news kids can see that we're living in a violent world, where adults murder, rape, and steal from one another on a regular basis. Real life is far worse than anything Hollywood or game manufacturers have to offer.

If real-life violence is the problem, would tougher gun laws prevent another Columbine?

Not really. Existing laws already state that guns cannot be sold to youths under eighteen, and Eric and Dylan found a way around that. Three of their guns were purchased at a gun show, with the help of a fellow student who was eighteen. Their TEC-9 handgun was bought illegally through a network of friends; the final transaction took place behind a pizza store.

No matter how strict the gun laws were, Eric and Dylan were determined to find a way around them. If people want to buy weapons illegally, it's only a matter of time before they succeed.

Did Eric and Dylan succeed in getting the guns because their parents weren't paying attention? Were the desire and the means to kill a result of parental negligence? After violent music and media, the parents are the next-favorite target of those looking for quick answers.

I can't speak for Eric Harris; I didn't know his family well enough to comment one way or the other. But I know Dylan Klebold came from a good home, with two loving parents who were far better to him than many other parents I know. It doesn't make any more sense to blame them than it does to blame Marilyn Manson.

Perhaps the answers lie a little deeper. Perhaps we have to look toward ourselves.

A human being is only that which he or she experiences. The human mind at birth is a "tabula rasa"—in other words, we come into the world with a blank slate. We learn from all that we see and hear, and this shapes our beliefs.

What Eric and Dylan saw happening in the real world shaped them more than any movie or video game. In my opinion, what they experienced in the real world is what we should be investigating.

Kids today are growing up in a world that can only be described as "the blind leading the blind." It's a world where parents, both of whom are working outside the home and wrapped up in their own lives, are leaving the upbringing of their children to public school teachers—who are unprepared both emotionally and logistically for such a feat—and television, where programs teach complicated, skewed morals that kids' young minds aren't yet ready to digest.

Kids are raised on the playgrounds of their schools, where they learn that "might makes right" and that physical brawn is a far more important asset than intelligence and cunning. Yet they also learn that when they fight back, they are punished by the people who are supposed to protect them and to dispense justice.

Dylan was harassed by kids who had never been taught why it's wrong to beat up another classmate, or whose own self-esteem was so crushed that they felt they had to destroy his, too, so theirs could be pumped up a little more.

The world, at its heart, has logical rules. Yet young people today are being taught that the opposite is true. Kids grow up in a world where they learn through experience that life is cruel, that their fellow human beings are mean-spirited bullies, and that basic questions about right and wrong are answered with rules that have no basis in reason other than "Because I said so."

As a result, they hunt for something else to believe in.

Dylan was a smart kid who could see the injustices of the world as clearly as I could. He was frustrated by them, and, like many other kids, he saw a bleak future for our generation.

Eric Harris felt much the same way.

Eric had been moved around all his life, and had known the difficulties of trying to fit in at one strange school after another. Like Dylan, Eric was exceptionally smart. And like Dylan, Eric saw the injustices of the world quite clearly, even as he was getting beat up in the high school locker room or jumping to avoid the glass bottles thrown at him out of the passing cars of Columbine football players.

The difference was, Eric had a dark side. He had a mean streak that was only fueled by the injustices he saw. He chose to take revenge, in the most destructive way he could think of—and once he had that solution in mind, he convinced Dylan that it was a revenge that was deserved.

Why? What made them cross that line? What made it possible for Eric to convince Dylan that they should murder thirteen innocent people? Why were Eric and Dylan's morals and ethics so depleted that they came to this point? Why were they capable of killing on such a grand scale?

These are the hard questions, and the answers do not come easy.

Yet, no matter how hard it may be to find those answers, we have to start the search. The fact of the matter is that school shootings are continuing to happen. We can just sit back and call the shooters "sick monsters, completely different from us," and decide that the problem will be solved by censoring music and violence in movies. Or we can accept that there are more Erics and Dylans out there, who are slowly being driven by society down the same path—and that if we act now, we can still reach them before it's too late.

This book represents a piece of closure on this chapter of my life. I'm finally getting my story out—a story of growing up labeled as an "outsider" in the school system, trying to get by each day in the face of cruelty and indifference.

It's a story of living in fear even before the killings, the object of Eric Harris's death threats. It's a story of being labeled a suspect by the police after I dared to suggest that they could have stopped the killings by acting on the information I'd given them.

It's a story of being powerless to get answers from the police once the investigation was underway, and watching as one lie after another emerged about that day.

Most of all, my story is one of growing up with a friend I thought I knew, then watching him become something I never imagined he could be.

My hope is that the people who read this will look at the big picture behind Columbine, and see where things need to change. I hope they recognize that they're not alone when they question what happened that day, or when they wonder what's really wrong with our society.

I hope that people will open their eyes.

3

LONG BEFORE ERIC HARRIS EVER ENTERED THE PICTURE, DYLAN Klebold was my friend.

We met at Normandy Elementary School. It was the first day of first grade, a time when school is something new and unexplored. We were young, wide-eyed kids, nervous and excited to be facing this grand new adventure. School, after all, is one of the first steps you take without your parents right there next to you.

Dylan was a shy kid. The first day of school, he pretty much kept to himself. Yet my parents had always taught me to give new people a chance. So it just seemed natural to go up to Dylan and say hello.

Once I'd coaxed him out of his shell, I found out that Dylan and I were pretty similar. For one thing, we were both diehard fans of video games. Both of us owned the Nintendo Entertainment System, the cutting edge of video games in 1987. We became friends right away.

Our circle of friends included a good handful of the boys in first grade. That year, no one thought about "jocks" and "geeks" and the other social cliques that would become dividers later on. Dylan and I were friends with Kevin Hofstra, who would grow up to be captain of the soccer team at Columbine. In first grade, friends are friends.

Like most people, my memories of first grade aren't exactly crystal clear. But I do remember it as a time where I felt like I belonged at school.

Brooks's parents, Randy and Judy Brown, cared a great deal about raising their children in a good environment. Randy worked in real estate, and purchased a house in the Jefferson County School District, which he had been told was "a great place to raise a family."

The Browns had two sons, Brooks and his younger brother, Aaron. At first, both seemed very happy at Normandy Elementary School; in fact, Brooks raved to his parents about Mrs. White, his first-grade teacher.

"Mrs. White was wonderful," said Judy Brown. "She really took care of the kids as if they were her own. Brooks loved her."

Judy also recalled the positive environment that White created for her son and his classmates. "What I remember most about Brooks from that time," she continued, "is that in the mornings, I would drop him off and the other kids would yell, 'Brooks! Over here! Over here!' Everyone liked him; he was the big kid that everybody wanted to play with, and he was nice to the other kids. He loved his teacher, and he loved school.

"The next grade," she said, "was where things started to change."

People will ask me what I remember the most about grade school with Dylan Klebold. Sadly, my strongest memory is of both of us kneeling on the floor of the Normandy Elementary School bathroom, bawling our eyes out as we took turns scrubbing a little girl's muddy jacket with a toothbrush.

It all started during recess. We were outside, playing in the leftover snow from a few days before. As we ran around, I found a big patch of ice that was starting to melt but was still plenty solid enough to play with.

"Hey, Dylan!" I said. "Come here!" By the time Dylan arrived, I was already bouncing and sliding on the slushy patch. Dylan gamely joined in, our feet smashing little spiderwebs into the ice as it buckled under our weight.

Dylan's boot crashed down on a corner of the ice and made the whole patch shift. It tipped into a puddle underneath, which splashed a good amount of muddy water into the air. A girl in our class was standing nearby, wearing a brand-new coat her parents had just given her; the mud left a jagged brown stripe right down the front of it.

It was an accident. We hadn't thought the ice was going to do that. But our classmate took one look at her ruined coat and started screaming

The second grade teacher immediately ran over to assess what was happening.

"It was an accident," I tried to say. "We were just playing with some ice, and—"

"Don't you have any respect for other people's property?" I remember the teacher yelling at us. "Don't you? You two are coming with me right now."

Dylan and I knew we were in trouble, but at the same time, we didn't understand why the teacher was so angry. It wasn't as if we had thrown the mud at the girl, or stolen her coat and rolled it around on the ground. Maybe we'd been a little careless, but that's all. It was still an accident.

We tried to get the teacher to listen to us, but she ordered us to be quiet as she carried the girl's coat into the bathroom.

Both of us were bawling by the time she had us at the sink, wetting a toothbrush. She put the coat in Dylan's hands. "I want this cleaned!" she ordered. "You two will stay in here and scrub that mud off, and you're not leaving until I say you're finished!"

Choking back our tears, we took up the brush and started working. We quickly discovered that using a toothbrush on mud wasn't very efficient—but we didn't have any choice. Both of us continued to cry, our ears burning red from the embarrassment of being yelled at, of our teacher's spiteful glare, of people looking at us as we worked.

"It's not coming out!" Dylan kept saying, rubbing the same spot for what seemed like the 500th time.

"We have to get it," I remember saying in response. I just kept repeating that. "We have to get it."

Judy Brown happened to visit the school that day to drop off something for her son during lunch hour.

"I was in the hall, and I ran into the teacher and she was red-faced mad," Judy recalls. "And I said, 'What's going on?' She said, 'Your son and Dylan ruined this girl's coat. He is in the bathroom right now, trying to clean it.' I asked when this had happened, and she said it had been over an hour before. She went and got Brooks to have him talk to me, and when he came out, he was in tears.

"So I took her aside, and I said, 'You know what, you're going a little too far with this,' " Judy continued. "I talked to Brooks and he said that he wanted to stay in school, that everything was okay. Well, I went to pick him up after school, and guess what? She had made them stay in there for the whole day, and now she was keeping them after school as well. She wasn't going to let it drop. This teacher was out of control, and it was over mud."

To this day, Judy is angry about the treatment of her son and his classmates in second grade, and not just because of the bathroom incident. "She expected these kids to be perfect," she says today. "And kids aren't perfect. But she would have none of it. She absolutely terrorized my child."

Scrubbing a coat in the bathroom may not have been such a bad thing by itself, but it was kind of the icing on the cake. Second grade had, from the beginning, been completely different from first grade. For Dylan and me, it was the first time in our young lives that we felt like an adult hated us.

The teacher would single out the kids who she caught picking their noses in class, and openly mock them in front of everyone. She would yell at us, especially the boys, for almost any infraction. Some teachers are nicer to boy students or to girl students. It was clear where this teacher's preferences lay.

The teacher also frightened many kids with an ill-timed story about bees. Our second grade class met in a temporary structure outside of the main Normandy Elementary building. A bees' nest was in the trees near-by, so it wasn't unusual to see the insects buzzing around as we walked by each day.

One day, our teacher chose to read to us a book called *A Taste of Blackberries*. It was a Newberry Award winner, which is probably why she picked it. Still, it scared us, because it involved a kid who dies from a bee sting.

For months afterward, Dylan and I were afraid of that bees' nest, and we weren't the only ones. One of the girls was terrified, because she was allergic to bees. Kids had everything from apprehension to outright terror on their faces as they walked to class each day, watching those insects out of the corner of their eye.

A few times, I told my parents about what was happening in school. It was the first time I ever remember hearing my father use the word "bitch." My parents tried to complain to the principal about the teacher; however, nothing was done.

So when the chance came to leave Normandy Elementary and join the accelerated program at another school, Dylan and I didn't voice any objections.

By the end of second grade, Dylan and I had joined the Cub Scouts, building Pinewood Derby cars and having "den meetings" every month. It was at one of these meetings that my parents first met the Klebold family.

Tom and Sue Klebold were the type of parents who made their children a top priority. In addition to Dylan, they had an older son named Byron, and the Klebolds made it a habit to attend every activity their kids were involved in. If Dylan and Byron were involved in different activities on the same night, then one parent would go to Dylan's activity and the other would go to Byron's. They were always involved in their sons' lives. To this day, when I hear people ask questions like "Where were the parents?" when it comes to Columbine, I cringe. The Klebolds were excellent parents to Dylan and Byron.

It was Tom Klebold who fought to make sure Dylan got into the accelerated learning program in the first place. He had technically tested high enough, but organizers were worried that there weren't enough female students who'd made the cut. So when Mr. Klebold heard that Dylan was going to lose his spot, he stepped in. His son wasn't going to be denied what he'd earned because of politics, Mr. Klebold said, and he made sure administrators corrected the problem.

The Klebolds originally hailed from Ohio. Mr. Klebold worked in the oil and gas industry; his job moved him first to Oklahoma, and then to Lakewood, Colorado. Shortly after Dylan was born, the Klebolds came to Littleton. Soon Mr. Klebold began working in the mortgage management business, while Sue worked with disabled students at Arapahoe

Community College.

The Klebolds and my parents got along well, and my mother and Mrs. Klebold became close friends. I often saw them together, either when Dylan stayed over at my place or when I went to his.

The Klebolds discouraged violence in any form. Dylan told me once that he wasn't allowed to have any toy guns in the house. As we got older, his mom worried about the level of violence in the video games we were playing.

Our parents' friendship was a bonus for Dylan and me; it made it easier for us to spend time together. On weekends at each other's houses we played board games, built castles out of Lego blocks, and battled each other on Nintendo. Dylan was a master at the game *Ninja Gaiden*; I could never keep up with him.

We also discovered the joys of chasing crawdads at the creek near my house. Dylan would come over, and we'd grab a couple of jars and head down to the creek. When we'd caught a few crawdads, we'd put them in our terrarium and keep them for a few weeks. Sometimes our moms would take us to the park together; the adults would sit on benches and talk while Dylan and I chased frogs.

My mom has a picture of Dylan and me at the state Capitol in downtown Denver. I'm pointing to the building, and Dylan is standing next to me, grinning. We were mighty third-graders in the big city, and we were ready to conquer the world.

I couldn't have asked for a better pal in grade school than Dylan Klebold. In fact, my mom still has a drawing of the two of us that I made in class; underneath it, I wrote in crayon, "What scares me most is if Dylan does boast that he isn't my friend."

❖

"Dylan was the sweetest, cutest kid you'd ever meet," said Brooks's father, Randy. "He was really shy, though, and it would take him fifteen or twenty minutes to warm up to us every time he came over, even though we knew him and we were close to him. After he'd warmed up, he was okay."

Judy Brown remembers Dylan Klebold as "a sensitive, caring child" who worried a lot about what other people thought—perhaps too much for his own good. She recognized the way that Dylan seemed to internalize what was bothering him, rather than being open about it. It was a familiar problem.

"I raised my kids to be extroverts, because I was an introvert when I was younger and I never wanted them to go through what I went through," she said. "When they were little, I would take them to parks and they would go over and talk to the adults they saw. I would always say to them—and maybe I shouldn't have said this to Brooks so much—'Loud and proud.' I wanted to teach them to speak up.

"That was just something Dylan could never do," she said. "I used to be the same way, never telling anyone what was bothering me. Ever... As Dylan got older, he never told his parents he was teased. Never. He kept it all inside."

The accelerated learning program for students in the Jefferson County Public Schools is called CHIPS, or "Challenging High Intellectual Potential Students." Its intent is to push advanced kids to the next level. Classes took place not at Normandy Elementary, but at Governor's Ranch Elementary a few miles away. We were promised advanced learning classes, regular field trips to educational spots all over the state, and an education that would put us well ahead of the rest of the pack by the time we got to junior high.

Dylan and I both got in. So did a few of our friends from Normandy. Our parents congratulated us. They were proud to see their boys test high enough to move to the next level—and we felt pretty good about it, too.

What we didn't know at the time was that admission into CHIPS was based on politics as much as ability. Some kids got in because they tested high enough on the entrance exam; other kids got in because of who their parents were. Naturally, parents in Jefferson County wanted to be able to say that their child was in "the accelerated program," and some parents had friends in the school district, or were otherwise in a position to pull a few strings.

As a result, the CHIPS program wasn't a big group of accelerated kids who were there to better themselves. Instead, what you had was one group of kids who had earned their spots, another group of kids who hadn't—and all of them trying to one-up the others, each trying to prove that he or she wasn't one of the "free ride" kids.

If you did a class project, you had to safeguard it from kids who might smash it when your back was turned. When kids smacked each other in the back of the head during class, the teacher would look the other way. Once kids realized that discipline in CHIPS was nonexistent, they went wild.

Finding friends within the CHIPS program was virtually impossible. In complete contrast to the friendly atmosphere we'd had at Normandy, classmates in CHIPS weren't friends; they were competitors, and it was a battle to make sure that nobody got too far ahead of anybody else. There's a theory about "crabs in a barrel": when a lot of crabs are trapped together in a barrel, every now and then one of them manages to climb over the others and make it to the top. When it does this, the other crabs grab onto it and pull it back down. Classes in the CHIPS program worked in much the same way.

Looking to the other kids at Governor's Ranch for friendship didn't work, either. Every day at recess, the other kids knew who the CHIPS kids were. "Oh, there's the smart kids," they'd sneer. They hated our guts. Dylan and I got our first taste of bullying on the playgrounds of Governor's Ranch. It wouldn't be our last.

We had been put into a class that we'd thought would consist of intelligent kids and teachers who cared about us. What we got was the opposite, and we felt disappointed and hurt.

I could feel the experience making me meaner. In first and second grade, I never got into fistfights; now they were almost commonplace. I would even fight with my little brother, Aaron, who was two grades below me. I was spending every day defending myself from bullies on the playground and saboteurs in the classroom, and my aggression was boiling over.

Dylan was showing signs of it, too. One day, he and I got into a fight on the playground. He said something that made me mad, so I pushed him. Just like that, he jumped on me and started punching; we rolled around, locked together, until the teachers peeled us apart and sent us to the principal's office.

That fight was the first time I ever saw Dylan's temper. Because Dylan internalized things so much, he would let his anger build up within him until one little thing finally set it off. When that happened, it was like an explosion.

The funny thing was, we weren't even that mad at each other; we were still close friends, still sleeping over at each other's houses. Yet the day-to-day experience of school had us both on edge, to the point that we were as ready to lash out at each other as our tormenters were.

I didn't trust authority anymore. I didn't trust my classmates. I was having trouble even trusting my own friends. My anger spilled over into everything at Governor's Ranch, until finally I had to face an ugly truth:

I hated school, and everything about it, and I didn't want to be there anymore.

I had been a straight-A student in first and second grade. Now, as my grades started to slip, my parents could see that something was wrong. When they asked me what it was, I told them everything that had been happening.

At first, they thought I was just having trouble adjusting, but they soon realized that the problem ran deeper. They began looking into alternatives.

As it turned out, Byron Klebold was attending a nearby school called John L. Shaffer Elementary. The Klebolds recommended the school to my parents, noting that it had one of the top ratings in the state and that Byron was very happy there.

When my parents pulled me from Governor's Ranch at the end of the year, I was thrilled. I was the lone dropout from the third-grade CHIPS program, and proud of it; I was off to a new start at a new school.

Dylan, however, stayed behind. I wonder sometimes why he never wanted to come along, considering that his brother was there and he was so unhappy with CHIPS. Chances are, he knew how much it meant to his parents to see him in the advanced placement program.

He wouldn't have wanted to let them down.

4

video games

IT WAS THURSDAY AFTERNOON, AFTER ANOTHER LONG DAY IN SIXTH grade. Dylan, my little brother Aaron, and I were taking our usual thirty minutes of video game play in front of the TV.

This had become a tradition for the three of us, now that I was at Shaffer Elementary. Dylan's mom was still at work for the first few hours after school, so my mom would pick Dylan up and bring him over to my house. When Mrs. Klebold got off work, she came over and joined us.

Today, though, we were treating our video games far more seriously than usual. After all, we had just acquired a new title: *Mortal Kombat*.

The concept behind *Mortal Kombat* is simple. It's a martial arts fighting game. The player chooses from eight different warriors, all of who have come to the "Shaolin Tournament" for different reasons. Scorpion, the undead ninja, is seeking revenge on his opponent, Sub-Zero; Johnny Cage is the martial-arts movie star; Sonja, the American fighter, is chasing after arch-criminal Kano; Liu Kang is seeking honor for his family, and so on.

Mind you, these plot details don't matter much in the grand scheme of things. All that matters is that you beat the crap out of the other guy before he beats the crap out of you. The player who takes two rounds out of three is the winner of the fight.

Aaron and I had saved up our money for weeks to buy *Mortal Kombat.* We'd even found the "blood code" for the game in one of our gaming magazines. If you entered the right button combination at *Mortal Kombat's* title screen, it would enable blood to fly from your opponent every time you connected a punch, making the game seem far more "adult," like an R-rated movie.

Now it was finally ours. We had the manual sitting there in front of us, stating the button configurations for each move the characters did. From Johnny Cage's Splits to Liu Kang's Fireball, we had the moves memorized before we even started playing. I chose to play as Scorpion. Aaron chose Sub-Zero. Dylan chose Kano. We were ready.

By now, Mrs. Klebold had arrived at the house. My mom started the timer for our thirty minutes, and then she and Mrs. Klebold left us to it.

Only two can fight at a time, so the three of us constantly rotated: the winner of a round took on the person who had sat out the last round. Unfortunately, this meant that my brother stayed in the game while Dylan and I keep trading off. Aaron was two years younger than us, and it drove me crazy to get beaten so regularly by my little brother. But we still played relentlessly. After all, we wanted to see something never seen before in a video game: a fatality.

The fatality was a new concept, introduced in *Mortal Kombat.* After one player won two rounds out of three, the screen went dark. In a deep, sinister voice, the game instructed the player to "finish him." The player would have about two seconds to hit the right button combination; if he hit it in time, then the winner would do a special "trick" to finish off the other character.

We didn't know what the trick would be, of course; we were only ten and twelve years of age. The instructions didn't tell us.

My brother was the first to pull it off. After beating Dylan, Aaron quickly nailed the combination. We watched as Sub-Zero reached over, grabbed Kano's head, and ripped it from his body, complete with the gruesome sound of tearing flesh. Sub-Zero then held the dripping head aloft in triumph—the spine dangling from the now-severed skull—as bonus points piled up under Aaron's score.

We burst out laughing.

Not far away, my mother and Mrs. Klebold were having a conversation about the new violent video game that their sons were playing.

Mrs. Klebold—the same mom who wouldn't let Dylan play with toy guns—had reservations about *Mortal Kombat*. She was scared that this violence might affect us in a negative way. She thought maybe she should take the game away.

My mom was concerned as well. Aaron and I had been brought up in a very nonviolent home. When we were younger, my parents watched movies before we could, then noted where the violent scenes were so they could fast-forward through them whenever we were there. In fact, one time my dad fell asleep in front of the TV during the movie *Beetlejuice*, so my brother Aaron wound up seeing the scenes that my mom had deemed "too scary." My mom really let my dad have it over that.

Now, though, we were older, and my mom was learning to loosen the reins a little. She suggested that she and Mrs. Klebold listen to us while we played. They would decide what to do about the game based on our reaction.

We were laughing.

There was blood dripping from Kano's spine, and skin flaps hanging from his severed head. A pool of blood was forming on the ground.

We weren't traumatized. We weren't crying. We were laughing—and we didn't feel bad, not one bit.

Why? Why did three boys laugh at such a disturbing death? Why were young boys all over the nation laughing? Was this, as some would have you believe, really the beginning of the fall of Dylan Klebold?

Mortal Kombat represented the beginning of violence as a selling point in video games. After the success of that game, publishers went crazy with blood and gore. From *Doom* to *Postal* to *State of Emergency*, all violent-themed games owe something to *Mortal Kombat*.

Today, thanks to what happened at Columbine, many of these games are under fire from the pro-control, anti-thought politicians. They believe that since Eric and Dylan played *Doom* and then went on to kill people, *Doom* was in some way responsible for their actions.

In the halls of Columbine, Eric and Dylan set out pipe bombs in specific spots, in close proximity. Their goal was to have one blow up and start a chain reaction through the east side of the school. How do I know that? Because that's how you kill your opponent in *Duke Nukem*.

They walked in with their TEC-9 and Hi-Point assault rifle, shooting wildly. They thought this would work because it works in *Duke Nukem*.

I won't dispute the idea that some of the elements of their plan were derived from video games. What I disagree with is the notion that video games *caused* the shootings—as well as most of the rest of the violence that takes place in America.

There are two basic types of video game players: those in touch with reality and those outside reality. Those who are in touch with reality represent the vast majority of players. We are the ones who, after work, go home for a few rounds of our favorite game, or who sit for hours and try to figure out parts of a new level. We're even the kind you see sitting on sidewalks in front of stores at midnight, waiting to purchase the latest system the moment it's released. We just prefer the hands-on nature of video games to the mindless nature of television.

However, there's that small segment of society that loses touch with the line between fantasy and reality. They are the ones who get into these games to such an extent that they believe there is some element of reality in them. You've seen these guys, dressed in capes with wands, wearing Klingon masks, and speaking of the characters as if they were real people.

Eric and Dylan both fall into this category. Their delusions went beyond capes and spells, and spilled into more serious things.

However, that doesn't make their actions the fault of the video games they played. Video games may have given them a place to direct their rage—but something else caused their rage in the first place. Something caused them to cross the line of fantasy and embrace imaginary worlds like *Doom* and *Duke Nukem* as an alternate reality.

When Eric and Dylan got into the world of video games, they loved it, because it was a world with definite rules. Those rules were preset, and they could not be broken. For a young man in a world like ours, it was a godsend. In the real world, the rules change constantly—and you could be in trouble at a moment's notice. But video games are different.

In a video game you only get what you know; nothing changes. So video games are a sort of haven, an escape to a logical, exciting world where two things are certain: justice is done, and you get what is due you based on your actions. Everything happens through your own doing, your own mistakes, and your own achievements.

Eric and Dylan got sucked into this appealing fantasy because it was an escape from the troubles of everyday life. When you have a place to go—whether it be home, school, a bar, a drug den, or a video game—where things seem perfect, then you go to that place as much as you can. It's a type of drug—a fantasy—where happiness exists because things make sense.

In real life, things didn't make sense. We saw our classmates being beaten by their parents, who were supposed to love them and nurture them. We heard our friends talking about how much their mommies hated their daddies—kids turned into bargaining chips in custody battles they couldn't even begin to comprehend. We saw racism, sexism, and cultural oppression—not just on TV or on the Internet, but in our own daily lives. These came from the adults we looked up to. These came from the world that we'd become a part of someday.

Kids are lied to by the people in power on a regular basis, whether it's in school or in politics. Our generation has come to know injustice as a way of life. Kids every day drop out and move on because they've come to believe that there are no fixed standards, and no reason for hope.

We can laugh at a virtual bloody skull, complete with severed spinal cord, on our video game screens. We know it isn't real. We know it's a work of imagination.

It isn't so easy to laugh at the horrors of the real world.

Shaffer Elementary proved to be a big improvement over where I'd been. In some ways, though, it was still tough; it's never easy to attend three schools in three years, and by the time I arrived at Shaffer, most kids had already formed their groups of friends and didn't pay too much attention to me. It wasn't the constant bullying and cruelty that Governor's Ranch had been, but it was lonely.

My grades didn't improve. My previous experiences had soured me on school, and I had started to tune it out. It wasn't that I couldn't handle the work; I was still getting A's on the assignments I turned in. The thing was, I'd only turn in half my assignments. If you get three A's and two incompletes, your average score drops down to a D real quick.

My parents and I began fighting about my grades. It didn't help when I took the Iowa Test of Basic Skills—a multiple-choice standardized quiz that kids all over the country take every year—and scored in the 99th percentile. My parents would look at that, then look at the C's and D's on my report card, and demand to know why I wasn't "working to my potential."

My answer would always be simple.

"Because I hate school."

"Brooks was grounded a lot," said Randy Brown. "There was one program where the teachers would call us and say, 'Brooks didn't do his homework this week,' and he'd get grounded. We hoped that would get him to shape up. It didn't.

"It drove us nuts because his behavior was so self-defeating," he continued. "I could never figure out what his problem was. The more we would push him, the less he would do."

However, the Browns weren't the kind of family that left the education of their sons completely to the school system. Both parents would read to the boys every night; while Judy read them children's classics or stories about history, Randy challenged them with more advanced litera-ture like Cyrano de Bergerac and excerpts from Les Miserables.

They also would make it a point to teach the boys a new vocabulary word each week. This led to some comical moments at school.

"My favorite story was what happened to Aaron in first grade," Judy said. "The teacher said, 'Okay, class, I need words that have the short vowel sound 'a.' So she's going on with 'cat,' and 'bat,' and 'hat.' And Aaron raises his hand and says, 'How about 'anomaly?' The teacher couldn't believe it. As the kids got older, we bought the Word Smart book and did a page a night at the table.

"Most important, though, was that we wanted them to have a sense of culture," she added. "We took them to high school plays. We'd take them to the Events Center, or to the touring companies of Broadway

shows that came through town. We went to Peter Pan, Phantom of the Opera, Les Miserables ... *We thought it was important that the boys learn about the good things in the world."*

In the fall of 1993, I started junior high at Ken Caryl Middle School. It meant a reunion with many of my old classmates from Governor's Ranch—and a major increase in the aggression that had been cultivated there.

Dylan and I were at the same school again. Yet we hardly saw each other, because students at Ken Caryl were divided into three groups, or "cores." In seventh grade, you had cores 7A, 7B, and 7C. If you were in core 7A, you'd hardly ever cross paths with the kids in 7B. Dylan and I were in different cores. We might as well have been at different schools; I'd see him outside occasionally, but that was it.

Junior high was difficult, because the bullying had become worse. I got beat up a lot, especially by the athletic kids. Their reason was simple: I wasn't one of them. It's not like I didn't try; I even played basketball for the Ken Caryl team in seventh grade. I liked baseball and soccer, and sometimes I'd get in on football games if one got going on the field. But I didn't fit in with the mentality of the "jocks." They didn't like me, and they refused to accept me into their groups. They preferred to just push the different kids around.

I went through a period of trying to be what I thought other people wanted me to be—a person they would like and accept. I started bragging about myself, making up whatever I thought might make people like me. I'd tell people I had tested with a really high IQ, or I'd lie about how many miles per hour my fastball was. It was a stupid thing to do, but when you want friends, sometimes you try to paint yourself as someone other than who you really are. You watch what other people are doing, you figure out what's "cool," and you adapt accordingly.

Of course, it made no difference. So I decided to try and fight back. One time during recess I was being made fun of by this kid named Jeremy and a group of his friends. They followed me around, calling me "faggot" and making fun while I tried to play football at recess. They'd reach out and trip me, or kick me when I wasn't looking, and then laugh about it.

When I'd had enough, I followed him and said, "Hey, Jeremy, turn around." He did, and I punched him in the nose as hard as I could. He fell down, but his friends immediately jumped on me. Needless to say, I took a pretty bad beating —and afterwards, as I was walking to the office, the other kids laughed and pointed at me, calling me a "pussy."

Teachers would punish any kid who was involved in a fight, no matter who had started it. One time I was in the locker room after gym class when, without any provocation, a kid came up and kicked me square in the crotch. I immediately dropped to the ground, while my friend Matt Cornwell jumped on the offending kid and started throwing punches. All three of us wound up in the office.

Even though all three of us told the same story—the first kid even admitted that he'd kicked me first—all three of us were punished. I received a suspension simply because I'd been involved, even though I'd never thrown a single punch. Matt got an even bigger suspension because he'd defended me. You really begin to resent those in authority when things like that happen.

By eighth grade, I had started hanging out with kids in the "punk" crowd. The punk kids accepted me. They felt like outcasts, just as I did, and they identified with music that attacked the establishment and the majority. I also noticed that when you have friends around you, the bullies don't pick on you as much. They might still call you names as they walk by, but they won't gang up on you and start hitting you. School felt like a prison yard, in a way: you find a "gang" of people to hang out with so that the other "gangs" leave you alone.

My grades dropped further, alarming my parents. We started fighting more and more. I just didn't care anymore—not about grades, not about my future, and definitely not about school. I was involved in a few extracurricular activities, like basketball at the YMCA and working with the disabled kids at school, but more and more, I started to drop out of them. By eighth grade, all I wanted was to hang out with my friends— friends that my parents really didn't approve of.

I did things to escape from my problems. I worked on computers. I played video games. I disappeared into books. Anything seemed better than the real world.

Dylan and I spent little time together during junior high. Not only were we not in the same classes, he wasn't part of my crowd. While I rebelled, frightening my parents, Dylan kept his anger inside and focused on being a good student. He didn't really come over to my house anymore, and for a while we lost track of each other.

However, Dylan was as much a target for the bullies as I was. He was still internalizing his anger and pain, escaping into computers or video games rather than deal with the troubles he faced. But that escape doesn't last for long. Eventually, the player must return to the real world—and when Dylan did that, the treatment he received from his classmates affected him deeply.

It wouldn't be until high school that I would learn just how much.

5

freshmen at columbine

I CAME TO COLUMBINE IN THE FALL OF 1995, BELIEVING IN MY HEART that school was going to get better. All through junior high, all I had heard about were the opportunities at Columbine—the activities, the teachers, and the chance to learn about bigger and more adult things. New kids, new beginnings, and a new school. I had so much hope.

We arrived at a new Columbine, so to speak. During the summer of 1995, construction crews had torn down much of the school and performed a $15 million renovation on it. Our class, the class of 1999, would be the first to enter and graduate from the newly refurbished building.

That fall I met Eric Harris for the first time.

My friend Nick Baumgart had decided to make a haunted house out of his garage for Halloween. I'd known Nick since grade school, and we'd become friends again at Columbine, so when he asked people to come over and help, of course I pitched in.

Dylan came along, and he had Eric with him. I also met Zach Heckler, who like us was really into computers. In fact, a whole lot of people came out. It was just a silly haunted house, but everyone wanted to be a part of it. We were crazy freshmen looking for something cool to do.

I talked to Eric a little that night. The next day, I went to the bus stop and saw him there. He only lived a few blocks away from me; it turned out that we'd been riding the same bus and just hadn't really had much reason to talk until now. Besides, Eric didn't ride every day. He would snag rides from his older brother whenever he could, because no one wants to be "one of the losers riding the bus." But over the next few weeks, he and I started hanging out regularly.

Unlike Brooks and Dylan, Eric Harris did not grow up in Colorado. In fact, his family moved several times during his childhood. He was born on April 9, 1981, the second child of Wayne and Kathy Harris. Two years later, the family would move to Dayton, Ohio; by the time Eric was in third grade, they had relocated to Oscada, Michigan. When Eric was in sixth grade, the Harrises moved again, this time to Plattsburg, New York; a little over a year later, when Plattsburg Air Force Base closed, Wayne Harris retired from service and moved the family back to his native home of Colorado.

From most accounts, it was hard for Eric to leave his friends behind each time he moved. Ken Caryl Middle School in Littleton would be the seventh school he had attended since kindergarten.

Eric and Brooks never spoke at Ken Caryl, although Eric and Dylan became friends. Both loved computers, video games, and baseball. However, it would not be until their high school years that Eric and Dylan would become inseparable. Both were computer-savvy, both felt like outcasts, and both knew the pain of bullies and rejection.

Also, both were quickly rejected by the establishment at Columbine.

Eric's older brother Kevin was a kicker for the Columbine football team. Kevin had always been friendly toward us. He was technically the "jock" in the family, and he'd give us a hard time about being freshmen, but it was always good-natured. Kevin was on the football team because he loved the game. It wasn't about status.

I've always enjoyed sports, but not the mentality that seems to go with them. I played basketball in junior high and enjoyed going to professional sports games with friends. Sometimes Dylan would talk to me about the fantasy football leagues he played in. The games themselves are great—I can relate to the excitement and the competition. But what I don't relate to are the people who equate sports with status. "I am a football player, and therefore I'm better than you." "I am a basketball player, and therefore I deserve to make out with all the cheerleaders. Pathetic geeks like you are not on my level." I couldn't understand that. I didn't see any reason to play a sport other than pure love of the game. Too many people at Columbine seemed to be playing for other reasons.

I don't mean to imply that all jocks in the world are jerks. I've known athletes who are good people. The thing is, Columbine's culture worshipped the athlete—and that unconditional adulation had a pretty bad effect on many of the jocks at our school.

Eric shared my opinion on that. That's why he didn't play for the Columbine soccer team, even though he loved soccer.

Yet Eric loved his brother, and he loved going to games during our freshman year to watch Kevin play. Some have suggested that there was some sibling rivalry there, since Kevin was a football player and Eric hated football players, but I never noticed any problems. There we were, cheering in the stands—and Eric was cheering as loud as the rest of us.

During freshman year, we formed a circle of friends that included Zach Heckler, Nick Baumgart, Eric, and Dylan. Our favorite place to hang out was the Columbine library.

The library was a great place to trade jokes, or sit and talk about how much we hated the school. Conversations like those were nothing unusual. But we'd have fun, too.

Nick earned himself a reputation early on as the clown of Columbine's Class of 1999. We quickly discovered that he would do virtually anything for money, no matter how stupid or humiliating it was. Once we paid him to make an ass of himself in the library by hitting on a girl he liked.

Usually this money would be no more than the couple of quarters that we could scrape together at the time, but for Nick, it was the principle of the thing. He didn't really care about the money; he just knew that he could make people laugh, and that it was his "designated role" at Columbine to be the clown. So he filled that role with a flourish.

Sometimes we would get so rowdy with our jokes that we'd get kicked out of the library for the rest of the day. Most of the time, though, we did our best to avoid causing trouble. After all, our favorite thing was using school computers to surf the Internet, and we didn't want to lose that privilege.

Freshman year was the best, because there were relatively few restrictions. In 1995 the Internet was still a relatively new trend, and school officials didn't know that much about what was on it. So the monitors didn't pay any attention when we went to sites like InsaneClownPosse.com, Monty Python Online, or News Askew, filmmaker Kevin Smith's Web site. We'd get online and screw around all through study hall.

Sophomore year, though, they changed the policy on us. Now we had to have permission to be on certain sites, and we'd get in trouble if we were caught surfing one that wasn't "education-related." Our Columbine school ID cards had three "lights" on them: red, yellow, and green. The first time the teachers caught you going to a non-educational site, they punched out the green light on your ID and called you a "yellow-lighter." That meant you were "in trouble" and had a warning against you. If they caught you a second time, they punched the yellow light. That meant you weren't allowed to use the Internet for the rest of the year.

To enforce this policy, anyone using a computer in the school library had to put his or her ID card up on top of the computer monitor, so that the teachers on duty could see. That's not to say that you couldn't still go to "inappropriate" sites, though. I got away with it. You just had to be careful.

Computers were huge for us. Everyone is on the Internet now, but we were the kind of kids who were using it back when it was a "geek thing." All of us loved to sit on a computer and do nothing else.

I'd been into computers since I was a little kid, when my dad bought a Commodore. Most people don't even remember it, but it was a small, simple computer that you could learn programming on. So as a kid, I would sit and learn syntax code. I read books on computer programming, then tried to do it myself. As newer computers came out, like the Apple IIE, I got experience on them, and then in fourth grade my parents bought our first IBM.

Computers were one of the things that bonded us in our freshman year of high school. Nick was really into graphic design and working on Macintoshes. Eric was a video game nut who talked sometimes about designing games for a living. All of us lived for playing Sega Genesis or Nintendo, and we loved computer games like *Duke Nukem* and *Doom*.

Most people looked at computers then as a "nerd" thing. We were proud to be nerds. We could relate to the logical simplicity of a computer. It made sense.

What we saw happening at Columbine didn't make sense.

❖

It seems like once you get to high school, all of the social groups are decided within the first few weeks. Once they've solidified, the cruelty begins.

Sometimes kids would just ignore us. But often, we were targets. We were freshmen, and computer-geek freshmen at that. At lunchtime the jocks would kick our chairs, or push us down onto the table from behind. They would knock our food trays onto the floor, trip us, or throw food as we were walking by. When we sat down, they would pelt us with candy from another table. In the hallways, they would push kids into lockers and call them names while their friends stood by and laughed at the show. In gym class, they would beat kids up in the locker room because the teachers weren't around.

Seniors at Columbine would do things like pour baby oil on the floor, then literally "go bowling" with freshmen; they would throw the kid across the floor, and since he couldn't stop, he'd crash right into other kids while the jocks pointed and giggled. The administration finally put a stop to it after a freshman girl slipped and broke her arm.

One guy, a wrestler who everyone knew to avoid, liked to make kids get down on the ground and push pennies along the floor with their noses. This would happen during school hours, as kids were passing from one class to another. Teachers would see it and look the other way. "Boys will be boys," they'd say, and laugh.

The problem was that the bullies were popular with the administration. Meanwhile, we were the "trouble kids," because we didn't seem to fit in with the grand order of things. Kids who played football were doing what you're supposed to do in high school. Kids like us, who dressed a little differently and were into different things, made teachers nervous. They weren't interested in reaching out to us. They wanted to keep us at arm's length, and if they had the chance to take us down, they would.

The bullies liked to propel paper clips at us with a rubber band. If a teacher saw you get hit, he or she did nothing. But as soon as you threw it back, or did something to defend yourself, you were done. The teacher would grab you and you would be in the office. We were the "undesirables," and the teachers were just waiting for an excuse to nail us. The bullies knew it.

Usually we didn't fight back. One thing we learned early on was that if we responded at all to what the bullies did, they'd do it more. Bullies want power. They want boosts to their self-esteem, and they think that if they can make you fear them, they've won something. That's the mentality that bullied kids have to deal with on an everyday basis. We knew that there was nothing we could do to stop them, but at least they wouldn't get anything out of it if we just ignored them.

Even so, the pain of bullying was taking its toll on us. Eric, especially, was a target. He had two strikes against him; the first was that he had a slight chest deformity. It wasn't that noticeable—it was just sunken in a bit—but when Eric would take his shirt off in P.E. class, the bullies were ready and waiting to mock him. Mocking a guy for a physical problem he can't control is one of the most humiliating ways to bring him down.

On top of that, Eric was the shortest of our group. The rest of us, as we got older, became well over six feet in height; Eric never did. He was small, he was a "computer geek," and he wasn't even from Colorado to begin with. He was as prime a target as the bullies at Columbine could have asked for.

Brooks's experiences were not unique. A year after the Columbine tragedy, research into the school's atmosphere was conducted by Regina

Huerter, Director of Juvenile Diversion for the Denver District Attorney's Office. Huerter's findings paint a disturbing picture of cruelty and indifference in Columbine's halls.

From October 14 to November 29, 2000, Huerter conducted interviews with twenty-eight adults and fifteen current or past students regarding their experiences with bullying at Columbine and how administrators responded to it.

Huerter's nine-page report was presented to the Governor's Columbine Review Commission on December 1, 2000. It contained numerous examples of assaults, racism, and other forms of bullying that witnesses say went on in the years before the Columbine murders.

"All students with whom I spoke, independent of their status at school, acknowledged there was bullying," Huerter wrote. "One identified the unwritten rules of survival in the school as: 'Don't screw with anyone who can beat you up, don't look at jocks in the eye, bump them, or hit on their girlfriend, and don't walk in the wrong area …' "

At the same time, Huerter noted "a strong perception from nearly everyone I spoke with that there was 'no reason to say anything about the bullying—no one was going to do anything.' Some students were just 'untouchable.' "

Huerter described an "overwhelming" sense that teachers responded only to bullying they had personally witnessed—and that when "certain parties" were involved, even these incidents were overlooked.

Students and parents who did report bullying often met with an unsatisfactory response. Among the examples Huerter mentioned in her report:

* *Two students repeatedly bullied a fifteen-year-old classmate in Physical Education class two years before the shooting. "The victim was repeatedly subjected to 'twisters,' a form of pinching and twisting the skin," Huerter wrote. "Although the class was in ses-*

sion, the teacher didn't acknowledge knowing what was taking place. Another form of bullying against this student, a practicing Jew, involved racial slurs and ethnic intimidation, including threatening by the bullies to 'build an oven and set him on fire.' Each time a basket was made during P.E. basketball, the bullies would state, 'that's another Jew in the oven.' They also wrote a song to torment the victim." The boy reported the bullying, and initially administrators confronted the bullies over their actions. However, the report states, the victim continued to be harassed for the next year and a half—and each time the new incidents were reported, "The counselor would bring the bully in to question him, the bully would deny the behavior, and they would let it go, telling the family, 'we're doing everything we can,' " Huerter wrote. "The victim states that 'they (the administration) did everything but call me a liar."

- One student told his parents he wouldn't go back to Columbine after an incident with "four or five football players shoving and pushing him, harassing him verbally and following him to his car." The boy's father called school officials, who did not return the call for six weeks. When an administrator did finally call back, he was very short and rude, the father recalled. The family pulled the student from Columbine and enrolled him in Heritage High School nearby. The student told Huerter that he still refuses to enter Columbine property to this day.
- "I was told by adults working in the district that they were afraid to speak up about school issues, including school culture and bullying behavior, because they feared losing their jobs," Huerter wrote. "All said bullying behavior was going on, that they did tell APs (associate principals), and nothing was done."

According to Huerter, several of the individuals she interviewed pointed out that deans, assistant principals, and principals were "often, if not always, coaches, or had a coaching background. This feeds a further perception that athletes were given preferential treatment by those deans or APs."

Students who weren't the main targets of the bullies did not always realize the extent of the problem. One former student Huerter interviewed "felt the cliques and bullying were just part of being in school. She doesn't believe that now."

When this young woman's sister started at Columbine, she went from straight A's to failing. The family didn't know about it for months, until finally a physics teacher called. The girl reported being unhappy in Columbine's atmosphere, so her parents chose to enroll her in another school instead. There, "she is again flourishing," and notes that kids at her new school are friendly regardless of what "cliques" they're in.

The older sister now works with teens from several different schools. "As they talk about their school experiences it has become apparent that bullying is not present in all schools—at least not to the degree she witnessed at Columbine," Huerter noted.

As for students like Eric Harris and Dylan Klebold, Huerter wrote that everyone she interviewed described the pair as "loners" and "often the brunt of ridicule and bullying. Although no one had specifics about when and the degree of bullying they received, most often it was about shoving, pushing and name-calling."

Even those who associated with Eric and Dylan were punished. A female student told Huerter that she was talking to Dylan Klebold in the school hallway during her freshman year. "After their conversation was over, one of the notorious bullies slammed her against the lockers and called her a 'fag lover,' " Huerter wrote. "Many students were in the area, but no adults. She did not report this to the administration. When I asked

*her why, she said that everyone told her 'it wouldn't do any good because
they wouldn't do anything about it.' "*

Some kids take refuge from bullies through their schoolwork. This
wasn't a solution for me.

I found myself at odds with the teachers on almost everything. I
remember when we were studying the book *Animal Farm*, by George
Orwell. The book deals with animals that rise up against their oppressive
owner and take over their own farm. From there, they try to establish
rules that give all animals equality, but the power-hungry pigs eventually
take over until, by the end of the book, they are every bit as oppressive
as the humans that came before them.

I felt that Orwell wrote the book as a criticism of socialism. However,
our teacher at Columbine wanted us to look at it as "socialism gone
wrong." She argued that the entire book is great, up until the point where
the pigs became dominant. In my opinion, the point of the book is that
things went wrong the moment the animals opted for socialism, and we
were being taught the exact opposite of the author's intent.

Ideally, in a place where free exchange of ideas could happen, I could
have argued that point without fear of repercussions. Instead, I kept my
mouth shut. I had already been taught what happens when students went
against the flow at Columbine.

On test days in my American Civics class, those of us who finished
early were allowed to use the rest of the class period for reading. One day,
after I'd finished a test, I pulled out a copy of *Atlas Shrugged*, by Ayn Rand.

The teacher approached me and picked up the book from my desk.

"What are you doing?" I said.

"I don't like Ayn Rand," she said. "I don't want her being read in my
classroom."

"You can't do that," I said. I was actually laughing. I couldn't believe it. "You're going to take away a book in American Civics class?"

She responded that I was disrupting other students who were taking the test. I just shrugged, knowing I wasn't going to change her mind. A few days later, I got my book back. But I never forgot. For kids who wanted to think for themselves and go outside the lines, Columbine High School was not the place to be.

Because Eric was riding the bus with me every day, we hung out quite a bit during freshman year. I liked him; not only was he smart, he had a twisted sense of humor. He also had unique ways of showing off his feelings.

There was a girl named Tiffany Typher who rode the bus with us, and Eric took her to Homecoming our freshman year. Unfortunately for Eric, it wound up being their only date; she didn't want to go out with him again after that. Eric was pretty bummed out, because he had liked her a lot. So he decided to play a prank on her as revenge.

We decided to use some fake blood left over from Halloween to give Tiffany a scare. As the three of us were walking past Eric's house, I started talking to Tiffany to distract her while Eric set his plan in motion. Then, once he was ready, he let out a scream.

Both of us turned in time to see Eric lying on the ground with a bloodied rock in his hand. His head and neck were covered in fake blood, and he was no longer moving; it looked like he'd bashed his own head in.

For a few seconds I played along, acting all concerned for my friend. Then I couldn't hold it back anymore and I burst into laughter. Eric did too, chuckling hysterically as he picked his bloodied self up off the ground. Tiffany told him that he was extremely immature, and stormed off to her house. Needless to say, Eric wasn't any closer to getting another date with her after that.

We were an obnoxious group of kids sometimes. We liked to rebel against the establishment, against our peers, and against our parents. We found that there was an enjoyment to be had in doing things differently, and shocking people. Obviously I would never cover myself in fake blood today. But at the time, we saw it as a funny way for Eric to get back at one more person who had rejected him.

All of us were finding ways to rebel, whether it was our clothes, our music, or our attitudes. For me, it was reading. I would spend class time reading books I had brought with me instead of paying attention to the teacher. Often I would get yelled at in class for doing this, but I didn't care. Other kids would make fun of the fact that I carried books around with me; for a while, my nickname became "Books" instead of "Brooks," as if reading for pleasure was somehow improper. I didn't care about that, either.

I was once asked in class to write something memorable about my childhood. I wrote about the moment I first read *Atlas Shrugged*. I identified with the idea that "Each man must live for his own sake, not sacrificing others to himself, or himself to others."

We were individuals, all of us, and we were proud of it. Other kids tried to make us feel ashamed for feeling different. We never did. Their words hurt us, and we lived in constant fear and hatred of our tormenters. But we were proud of who we were. When it came to getting through the day, that made all the difference.

6

troubles

FOR YEARS, MY PARENTS URGED ME TO FIND SOMETHING I COULD BE passionate about. I'd always tell them that I was passionate about computers and about books, but that never seemed to get them off my back about the constant string of C's and D's that I brought home from Columbine.

Whenever I found something really interesting at school, though, I threw myself into it. There were two things that fit this description for me at Columbine: the theatre program and the debate class.

My dad encouraged me to join the debate team. At first it just seemed like another class, so I thought, "Why not?" and signed up. But once I arrived, I discovered that I loved it. I loved being able to debate in a situation where the other person can't just say, "You're an idiot," and walk off. Instead, the two of you have to continue until the judges say you're finished, and then afterwards they tell you, "Okay, you were right and you were wrong." The judges don't know either of you, so their decisions are based solely on the arguments you presented.

I enjoyed that so much. When you argue with people in real life, no matter how rational you are, generally the other person says, "Well, kiss my ass, I know I'm right," and then walks off acting like he won. In debate, we actually had to prove our points.

Not only that, debate allowed a student to constantly improve. After a debate, the judges will fill out a form telling you everything that you did or didn't do right, and generally they will give you helpful hints. Also, during my freshman and sophomore years, I would approach the kids who did really well during competitions and ask them for pointers. All through high school, I did better at each tournament because of what they taught me.

Being in debate class automatically meant I was on the debate team. The competitions would take place on weekends, at locations all over Colorado. My freshman year, we took first place at the Jeffco Invite for Lincoln-Douglas Debates, which was an incredible feeling.

Lincoln-Douglas debates are the perfect exercise for the analytic thinker. For each issue I was assigned, I would have to prepare arguments for either side. I wouldn't know which position I would have to take in the debate until two minutes before the round. That's tough, because it means that even if your personal opinion falls on one side of an issue, you have to be able to argue the other side convincingly enough to defeat the person who is arguing the side that you agree with. It was exciting. It reinforced the idea that there is more than one way to think, and more than one side to any issue.

For someone like me, the debate team was a godsend. The only thing that matched it was drama class.

I didn't get along with most of my teachers, but it's amazing the power that a positive, caring teacher can have. My best experience with such a teacher was Sue Caruthers, Columbine's drama teacher.

Mrs. Caruthers—or "Mrs. C," as we usually called her—ran the most fulfilling extracurricular program I've ever been a part of. There were three different drama classes: Beginning Acting, Intermediate Acting, and Advanced Acting. I entered the classes with my friend Zach Heckler, and both of us were immediately hooked.

In drama class we learned how to design light plots, run a soundboard, or help with set design. We also performed small scenes in class to polish our acting skills. The idea was that students in this class would go on to participate in the Columbine theatre program, whether as actors or as tech crew members. Students would focus in one area or another, but most of us would do a little bit of everything.

The very first play I worked on was *Get Smart*, during the second semester of my freshman year. I played a student, and I had two lines. But I was also working as an assistant stage manager, and I helped build the sets. I loved the program, and participated in it all four years at Columbine.

Unfortunately, being an actor gave the bullies all-new ammo with which to target me.

Imagine seeing an attractive girl in the hallway who's in one of your classes, but who you've never really had the chance to talk with. Somehow, you get into a conversation with her. She seems nice, and you like her, and she's laughing and you're starting to get hopeful. Then a couple of football players come around the corner and say, "Hey, what the hell are you talking to her for, faggot? Do you actually think you have a chance with her?" And then they pick you up and push you into a locker, and you look like a pathetic weakling in front of the girl you were trying so hard to impress.

Such things were commonplace at Columbine. If a guy was acting in the Columbine drama program, he was immediately labeled a "drama fag." Not only was he not playing sports—which was what all normal guys were supposed to do at Columbine—but *he was into that fine arts crap!* The bullies found whatever weakness they could and went after it. I was a wuss because I wasn't in sports. I was gay because I liked theatre. Then when I was in debate, it was like, "Ooh, you must be smart, huh huh huh." Apparently, they thought calling someone "smart" was an insult.

Columbine students quickly found their roles and stuck to them. I found my role in the theatre; so did Zach Heckler. And when sophomore year rolled around, Dylan joined us. Dylan hadn't taken drama class like we had, but he had an interest in working technical stuff behind the scenes, so Zach showed him what to do. It didn't take long for Dylan to become a sharp soundboard operator.

Besides theatre, though, the rest of our activities weren't so good. As freshmen and sophomores, we were already into drinking and smoking and would get trashed at each other's houses, or even in the light booth during plays. Dylan, in fact, earned a nickname based on his favorite drink: VoDkA. The name would stick for years.

While speech and drama gave me something to sink my passion into, they didn't solve the problems I was still having at school—or with my parents.

My grades at Columbine were as bad as—if not worse than—my grades from junior high. It wasn't because I couldn't do the work. It was because I *didn't* do the work. My grade point average got a boost from classes I enjoyed, like drama and debate, where I got A's. But in some other classes, like math, I was bored out of my mind and tuned things out. I did well on tests, but my grades still suffered because I didn't do the homework.

I didn't see a point in it, didn't want to waste my time on the busy-work that constituted most of our assignments. There was no reason to do it other than earning a grade, and I didn't care about the grade. I would only do homework if I thought I would get something out of it.

This attitude drove my parents crazy. They tried everything, from grounding me to speaking with my teachers, to trying to help me with homework. They also offered to let me change schools, since they knew I was unhappy at Columbine.

Part of me wanted to get out. The problem was that all my friends were at Columbine. I didn't want to leave them behind.

Of course, I was still very much into the punk and alternative crowd, and my parents didn't approve of that at all.

My parents never really understood why I hung out with some of the kids I did. I tried to explain that it was because they were the most independent kids in the school.

However, many of my friends in the punk crowd didn't come from very stable home environments. A few of them were pretty messed up. They would talk all the time about the problems they had at home. I wanted to fit in with these guys. So I started exaggerating my own problems. I would play up the pressure my parents put on me to get better grades. We were fighting all the time, and venting about those fights to my friends only aggravated my feelings.

I felt my parents weren't attempting to understand me. Instead, they were trying to "fix" me—to get me back to the way I was in grade school, before all of the crap with CHIPS and the junior high bullies and other unpleasantness. But you can't always fix other people. They have to fix themselves. My parents kept trying to push me back to what they saw as the best sort of life for me. When I would rebel, they would try to fix me more, and in turn I would become even more rebellious. It was a terrible spiral.

I would run away from home a lot, staying at my friends' houses in an effort to keep away from my parents. I resented them for pushing me to "buy into the system" and start getting good grades, or conform to what everyone thought I should be. They seemed to want me to play the game. I didn't want to do that, so I dropped out of the game altogether.

I had my driver's license by the end of sophomore year, so I was one of the first kids in my group of friends to have a car. Obviously this made me pretty popular as a ride-giver. My dad had given me an older car to drive, and, like a lot of kids when they first get their license, I treated it with no respect at all.

One time, after I'd been grounded, I left with the car anyway and picked up a few of my friends. My dad came looking for me, and pulled up next to me ordering me to go home. I refused.

"Go home right now, Brooks!" my dad shouted.

Since his car was sitting in front of mine, I threw my car into reverse and floored the gas. I wound up driving backwards through our neighborhood at what I can only describe as a ridiculous rate of speed; I'm lucky I didn't kill myself and everyone else in the car. Eventually I got myself turned around and sped away, and my dad decided we were going so fast that he wasn't going to bother chasing us.

I went through a pretty rough time, where I pushed my parents to the absolute limit. Today I realize how much they must have loved me, to put up with me through all of that.

Loving, involved parents are so important for a kid. I fought with my parents over some of the stupidest things. I feel really bad about that now. Because I know, today, how much they shaped me. And in the years that would follow, they would become a strong anchor that got me through my troubles with Eric and Dylan.

Eric never followed the rest of us into the theatre, or into any serious pursuit of extracurricular activities at Columbine. He remained engrossed in his computer. That was his outlet for the frustrations of school.

Eric and I were still riding the bus home together at the beginning of sophomore year, before I got my car. He lived close by, and the two of us would go over to his house and play video games.

One thing Eric was really into was coding levels for *Doom II*. That was one of the great things about *Doom II*. With most games, once you beat all of the levels, that's it; there's nothing left to do except play the levels you've already beaten, and that can get boring. But with *Doom II*, you could buy a *Doom* editor that would actually allow you to design your own levels of the game, program them with as many enemies as you wanted, and then play them by yourself or with friends online. It was possible to program in your own types of enemies and your own sounds, move things around in existing levels, or build entire new worlds from scratch.

Eric loved the challenges the editing program presented. He loved programming and figuring out how to do things like matching textures or de-bugging a new level. He also liked creating challenges for his friends to beat. So when he created a new level, he'd invite me over to his house to give it a try.

I never built a *Doom* level myself, but Eric and I would sit around brainstorming ideas for them. It took a considerable amount of time to build a new *Doom* level from scratch, and even more time to work the bugs out.

Eric's early levels were small, like the ones he designed for "death-matching." These levels didn't have any computer-controlled monsters running around; they were basically empty rooms with weapons hidden everywhere. Eric would get online with his computer, and Dylan or somebody else would log on with theirs, and the two players would enter this level and hunt each other down. Every time one player killed the other, it counted as one point. The first player to get ten points, or twenty, depending on how the scorekeeping was set up, won the match.

He'd often get creative; one level, called "Hockey," was just that—opponents would chase each other down inside a hockey arena, complete with ice that your character would slide across if he walked on it. Another deathmatch level was based on *Mortal Kombat*, where there were no weapons and the two players would have to punch each other to death. Another level, which Eric simply called "Deathmatch in Bricks," was a giant room with sweeping staircases, spikes, dark caves, a flowing river, and a maze. On the walls of the level, Eric had pasted in his own e-mail address, so that if the level got traded to other players online, they could write to him with their thoughts.

However, as Eric's design skills improved, so did the complexity of his levels. By sophomore year, he showed me a complex two-level adventure called "UAC Labs." Unlike the deathmatch levels, "UAC Labs" was a one-player challenge that involved fighting through a massive complex loaded with demons and enemy soldiers. In addition to designing the map of the level itself, Eric had reprogrammed a few features of the characters; I'm pretty sure that for one in particular he had sampled in the booming shriek of the monster from the movie *Predator*.

After the attack on Columbine, plenty of "experts" took aim at *Doom* and other games as "training ground" for Eric and Dylan. So there were a lot of people who wanted to get hold of the levels Eric designed, to see if there was any foreshadowing of the shootings to be found in them.

In truth, there really wasn't. Many of Eric's levels were based on science fiction ideas. Here's the description of "UAC Labs" in the text file that went with the level:

After defeating the demons on Earth, you learn of a new terror. Phobos, where this hellish battle all began, has been taken over again! When you were fighting hell on Earth, the demon back-up crew decided to pay a visit to Phobos again. No problem, right? All the installations were already destroyed by you and the first attack right? Yeah, that parts [sic] right, but half the surviving humans from earth took refuge there! We just re-did the structures to fit our needs, and moved in again. Bad idea. Those gates were still active. Sooo aah, chalk up another kill for the demons. After the 2nd attack on Phobos, only 99% of the human population is left. Once you emerged from hell, you took the first ship you could to Phobos. Once again, there were no survivors. Now it's PAYBACK TIME! Those goddamned alien bastards are gonna get one helluva BFG blast up their FREAKIN ASS! You land on the other side of Phobos. Where the humans landed for the 2nd time. Your mission is to destroy the 2 main gates, and destroy the platoon of demons at the main teleporter from Phobos to Earth. Use the maps, you'll need them to find all the hidden secrets and doors. Beware of the 2 gates, the[y] ARE still active, and more demons might come through any second. The platoon guarding the teleporter out is VERY large, so beware. Good luck marine, and don't forget, KILL 'EM AAAAAL-LLL!!!!!

After the attack on Columbine, there were some *Doom* players who reviewed "UAC Labs" because of its notoriety. They criticized the hell out of the level—particularly the ending, where over a hundred different enemies come out of the walls simultaneously. "I'm not sure 5,000 rounds would be enough, let alone 500," groused one reviewer as he gave a walk-through of the level. Another reviewer on the "Realm of Chaos" *Doom* site said Eric had "flagrantly exceeded" the "Thing Limit."

What these reviewers failed to understand is that Eric didn't care about their rules. He made up his own. *Doom* was an escape for him into a world he understood; it was a reality far preferable to the miserable existence of school. Eric found himself truly at home there.

The bullying at Columbine continued, but during sophomore year, several of us got to know a group of "outcasts" at school who had found a way to fight back.

They were commonly known as the Trench Coat Mafia.

I cringe to use that term today, because it has such a stigma attached to it. In the initial days after the Columbine massacre, several TV news shows latched onto the idea of the "Trench Coat Mafia" like it was some sort of cult. Stories implied that the Trench Coat Mafia was a national organization, or that it had ties with the Neo-Nazi movement. To this day, references are made to the Trench Coat Mafia; I even heard the term used on the HBO show *Six Feet Under* not too long ago.

In reality, the Trench Coat Mafia was nothing more than a group of friends who hung out together, wore black trench coats, and prided themselves on being different from the "jocks."

Even the trench coats were more of an accidental thing than any sort of "uniform." The mother of one of its members, Tad Boles, bought a black coat for him as a present when she saw one on sale. Once he started wearing it, his friend followed suit because they liked the look.

While sitting at lunch one day, a few of the athletes were doing their usual routine, making fun of the kids they didn't like. They saw this group of kids sitting together, all wearing black trench coats, on a day when temperatures were in the eighty-degree range. One guy commented that with the trench coats, the group of "outcasts" looked like some sort of "mafia."

"Yeah, like a trench coat mafia," said another.

The term was supposed to be an insult. Instead, the group embraced it as a badge of pride. They were the outcasts, and, rather than be ashamed of it, they were proud of it. In fact, they wanted to fight back against their antagonists.

That was the flaw of the Trench Coat Mafia. They prided themselves on being the opposite of the jocks, but they weren't. All they did was spread even more hate. Just as the jocks would make fun of and belittle anyone who was different from them, so would the Trench Coat Mafia. They would just do it in the opposite direction. Jocks would beat the shit out of them and laugh, and then the Trench Coat Mafia would go beat the shit out of some preps. They were filled with so much hate for the jocks and the bullies of Columbine that they allowed themselves to turn into the very thing they hated.

That's not to say that the Trench Coat Mafia was made up of bad guys. They were a pretty diverse lot, and that made for some interesting conversation. Some were Wiccans, some were Satanists, some didn't proclaim any faith whatsoever. I sat with them at lunch a few times, and they were very accepting of me. It was the jocks they hated.

The feeling was mutual. Jocks would call the girls who hung out with the Trench Coat Mafia "sluts" and "Nazi lesbians." One day at lunch the jocks threw a bag full of ice water on a member of the group, which led to a fight outside. When security intervened, the Trench Coat Mafia kids wound up with three-day suspensions. The jocks who had started the fight were never even sent to the office.

Even so, the Trench Coat Mafia had chosen to take a stand against the bullying at Columbine. Most of them had already graduated and moved on by the time my senior year arrived. But their actions—and their acceptance—made an impression on Eric and Dylan. For the first time, they were seeing a group of outcasts who weren't taking the bullying lying down. For once they were seeing kids who dished it right back.

Neither of them would forget that lesson.

One member of the Trench Coat Mafia, Chris Morris, had taken a particular liking to Eric. Chris had a job working at Blackjack Pizza, a restaurant just a few blocks south of Columbine, near the Cooper 7 Theater. He urged Eric to apply there near the end of sophomore year; Dylan soon followed suit.

It was during their time at Blackjack Pizza that Eric and Dylan really started to become close. Before that, we had all been one big group of friends. Now, though, Eric and Dylan were forming a bond that was much stronger than what they had with the rest of us.

Employees at Blackjack Pizza had a fun way to pass the slower hours at work: setting off dry ice bombs outside the store. They would get the dry ice from Baskin Robbins and make crude "bombs" by placing a construction-zone cone over the ice, letting pressure build up and seeing how high they could shoot the cone into the air.

However, Eric and Dylan were introduced to far more powerful explosives that summer. At some point, they discovered recipes on the Internet for building pipe bombs using ordinary PVC pipe and powder from leftover fireworks. In a police interview conducted after the Columbine massacre, the former owner of Blackjack Pizza recalled one of them bringing a pipe bomb to work one day and showing it off to other employees. The owner immediately told him to get rid of it.

For Eric, pipe bombs were a whole new adventure, a way of playing God that was far more exciting than the virtual reality of *Doom*. This wasn't just a game anymore. These explosives were the real thing.

Early in junior year, my little brother and I were playing around on the computer. Zach Heckler had come over, and the three of us were hunched over the monitor with a new program when we heard a knocking on the window glass.

I looked at my watch. It was nearly three o'clock in the morning. Yet there, crouching outside, were Eric and Dylan, dressed completely in black and carrying a backpack. I couldn't believe it. We let them in, and they sat down and told us how they had snuck out and were "carrying out missions" in the neighborhood.

By now, Eric and Dylan had clearly bonded much more strongly with each other than with the rest of us. Working together at Blackjack Pizza, they had developed a lot of mutual interests that they hadn't shared before. Eric—who took German at Columbine and spoke it fairly well—had discovered Rammstein, a German metal band, and he and Dylan became fans. That fall, Eric had started wearing black, just like the Trench Coat Mafia. It wouldn't be long before Dylan adopted a similar attire.

Brooks's junior year was also Aaron Brown's freshman year. He hadn't seen Dylan around in some time, and it was a shock the first time he saw him in the halls of Columbine.

"He looked like a totally different person," Aaron said. "I was like, 'Brooks, is that Dylan?' I couldn't believe it. He was a lot taller than the last time I'd seen him. He was dressed in all black, looking down, kind of sad. He just had this attitude about him—you could tell that he was very unhappy. He wasn't being accepted at all."

At first I didn't find Dylan's behavior that strange. It just seemed like he was finding a new side to himself. In fact, it was sort of interesting to see Dylan rebelling—like me, I thought. It seemed to be good for him; he was becoming more assertive. I didn't share his interest in Rammstein—I thought their music was pretty one-dimensional and lame—but it struck me that perhaps the changes in Eric and Dylan were positive.

I knew nothing of their pipe bomb building. They never told me about it. They did, however, tell me of some of the "Rebel Missions" they were starting to undertake in the neighborhood.

"The Rebels" is the name of the Columbine sports teams. Eric had adopted the name to describe not only himself—he now went by the nickname "REB" both online and at work—but also the acts of "revenge" that he and Dylan had begun to perform.

Eric had spray paint cans and superglue, and he told us how he and Dylan would sneak over to people's houses and vandalize them, because the person had said or done something at school that had pissed them off. Perhaps Eric and Dylan would glue someone's doors shut, or write words on their front lawn. They did these acts not as Eric Harris and Dylan Klebold, but as REB and VoDkA, the Rebels.

I think the story that got me the most was the one they told about Halloween of junior year. That night, the two of them went up on the roof with a BB gun and took shots at little kids who were trick-or-treating. They said the kids would look around, all confused at what had hit them, but because Eric and Dylan were concealed in the darkness of the roof, they never knew. They told us about this over lunch, laughing like it was the funniest joke in the world.

The first few times I heard stories like that, I laughed, too—out of shock, not pleasure. After a while, I couldn't even laugh anymore. The Halloween story really bugged me. Even if someone could see the humor in pulling missions of revenge on the houses of people who acted like jerks at school, taking pot-shots at little kids on Halloween is just plain sick.

But Eric and Dylan didn't feel the need to explain their behavior. They were angry with the world, and that anger was beginning to show.

7

broken glass

IT DIDN'T TAKE MUCH ANYMORE TO SET ERIC OFF. BY THE WINTER OF junior year, I would learn that lesson firsthand.

It wasn't some massive fight that drove Eric and me apart, or a prank that got out of hand. Eric decided that he hated me because I didn't give him a ride to school.

When Eric was a freshman, he got rides from his older brother whenever he could. Now that Kevin had graduated and gone off to college, Eric was back to riding the bus all the time, because he still didn't have his driver's license. So he had started riding along with me instead.

I had become friends with a guy named Trevor Dolac through the Columbine debate program. He and I would alternate driving to school. One week, I would drive on Monday, Wednesday, and Friday while Trevor took Tuesday and Thursday. The next week, we would switch. Eric simply rode along.

However, as anyone who knows me will attest, I'm not exactly punctual. Since I didn't care that much about school, I'd oversleep or dawdle around in the mornings, which meant that I was almost always running ten minutes behind. Trevor never got too annoyed about it, but it drove Eric crazy. Every morning, for the entire drive to Columbine, all I'd hear was Eric complaining about how I needed to get my shit together.

One morning, I overslept again. Trevor called me, wondering where I was.

"Sorry, man," I said. "I'll be right over."

As I got dressed, the phone rang again. This time it was Eric. I knew what he was going to say before I even picked up.

I didn't need this, I thought. After all, I wasn't asking Eric to pitch in gas money. I was late all the time and by now, Eric knew it. He still chose to ask for rides from me anyway, right? So he knew what he was getting. I told him I was running late. I suggested that he find another ride.

Unfortunately for Eric, the bus had already left. He was pretty pissed off about it, and he started yelling at me over the phone about what a dick I was. I let him yell for a little while, then hung up.

A few minutes later I was at Trevor's house. "Eric's being a little bitch," I said as Trevor got in the car. "We're not picking him up today. We're just going straight to school."

We headed out of our neighborhood toward Pierce Street. A familiar truck pulled out right in front of us. Eric had enlisted his dad to give him a ride.

When Mr. Harris saw our car, he pulled over and we followed suit. Eric got out of his dad's truck and climbed into my backseat.

"You asshole!" he said. "I'm ten fucking minutes late already! My dad's pissed off at me. I can't rely on you for anything!"

I'd had enough. I turned around in my seat and stared hard at him. "Dude, that's it. I don't need this shit every morning. I'm not giving you rides to school anymore."

We arrived at school and went our separate ways. Usually, if I drove everyone to school in the morning, I provided a ride home as well. But that afternoon, Trevor and I took off from school without Eric. We never gave him another ride after that.

The next time Eric saw me at school, he refused to acknowledge me; I'd pass him in the hallways and say, "Hey, Eric," and he'd just glare. Once I realized that he was going to make an issue of what had happened, I became so annoyed that I stopped talking to him, too.

I heard through my other friends that Eric was talking shit about me. For the most part, I shrugged it off. However, it did concern me when I heard that Eric wanted to mess with my car.

I told my parents what was going on. It didn't surprise my mom that much. She had already developed a distrust of Eric Harris.

"Eric held grudges and he never let them go," Judy Brown said. "It was not normal behavior for boys. Boys usually speak up, say what they have to say, and that's that."

Initially, Randy and Judy Brown liked Eric, because he seemed like the most clean-cut of Brooks's friends. Most of them dressed and acted like typical members of the punk or alternative scene. Eric, by contrast, looked almost preppy.

"My main impression of Eric was driving down Elmhurst and seeing him in the window of his study every night, every time we drove by, on the computer," said Randy Brown. "The Harris's study is in the front of the house, and every time I went by, he was there. It was uncanny.

"You have to remember, too, that we were much more naïve then than we are now," Randy continued. "The things that would now be considered red flags ... at the time we just excused as 'teenage behavior.'"

The first time Judy Brown suspected something amiss was when Brooks came home and told her that Eric was refusing to speak to her son Aaron. Aaron had made a comment to Eric along the lines of "Hey, man, get a life; you're on the computer too much." It was meant as gentle ribbing, but Eric didn't take it that way.

"Brooks said that Eric now hated Aaron," Judy recalls. "I said, 'You've got to be kidding. Can't you smooth it over?' And Brooks said, 'No way, Mom. There's no smoothing it over. He won't change his mind."

The next time Judy became concerned about Eric Harris was after Brooks and Eric had quarreled over rides to school. Brooks came home and said he'd heard that Eric was looking to damage his car in some way, for revenge.

"I remembered how Eric had held a grudge toward Aaron before," Judy said. "I knew he wasn't going to let this one go either."

Shortly after Eric and I had our falling-out, Eric figured out a way to get two of his enemies with one shot. He and Dylan plotted a new "Rebel Mission" against Nick Baumgart.

Eric had decided he didn't like the way Nick laughed. It was ridiculous, but no more ridiculous than choosing to hate my brother for telling him to get off the computer, or hating me because I didn't want to drive him to school anymore. The same "clownish" traits that had made us laugh so hard at Nick's antics in the library during freshman year now had Eric hating him with a passion. Go figure.

Dylan and Nick had never been great friends, not even in grade school, and I imagine it wasn't hard for Eric to convince him to help with the plan.

Dressed in their usual black "mission clothes," Eric and Dylan crept over to Nick's house late one night. They put superglue in all of his door locks, then tried to set fire to all of the plants and bushes outside.

Then, the next day, Eric went up to Nick and said, "Man, I'm sorry about your house. I was talking to some people and I heard that Brooks did it."

Nick went home and told his mom, and she went off the wall about it. So my mom called her to explain that I couldn't have been involved.

For the first time, my parents' strict demands on me regarding school were about to pay off. Because I hadn't been doing a lot of my school-work, my teachers had begun sending a card home with me every week that indicated whether or not I had done my assignments.

That week, I'd missed some assignments, so I didn't have the card. My parents and I had a big fight, and I wound up grounded. I lost car priv-ileges and had to stay at home every night. As it turned out, one of those nights was the night that Nick's house was hit.

"I can guarantee you that Brooks didn't do it," my mom told Mrs. Baumgart.

"Why?"

"Because he was here at home, grounded."

Based on that, it was pretty easy to figure out who the true culprit was. If Eric had been angry with me before, now he was furious.

A few weeks after Eric and I stopped talking to each other, Trevor and I happened to be driving home from school in separate cars. Trevor was driving his car ahead of me when we pulled up to the stop sign near my house.

The spot was right next to the bus stop. Eric, who was riding the bus again, was throwing snowballs with other kids from school.

When Eric saw Trevor, he picked up a chunk of ice from where it forms over the gutter. He threw it as hard as he could at Trevor's car, denting the trunk. Then, without missing a beat, he picked up another chunk of ice and threw it at my car.

The ice smashed into my windshield; I heard it crack. It wasn't a large chip, but enough to make one of those little spider webs around it.

I was livid. I slammed on the brakes and leaned out of the car, yelling, "Fuck you! Fuck you, Eric! You're gonna pay to fix this!"

Eric laughed at me. "Kiss my ass, Brooks! I ain't paying for shit!"

I floored the gas down the remaining few blocks to my parents' house, went in and told my mom exactly what had happened. Then—seeing red—I went straight to Eric's place to talk to his parents.

I hammered on their front door, still furious. All I could think of was getting back at Eric. Mrs. Harris answered, and I glared at her. "I've got something to tell you about your son," I said.

She looked back at me, a little confused. "Okay …" She asked me to come in.

We sat down in her living room, and I told her everything Eric had been doing in the past few months. "Your son's been sneaking out at night," I said. "He's going around vandalizing things. He's threatened people. And just now he broke my windshield."

She didn't seem to believe me. She kept asking me to calm down. That only made me angrier.

"He's got liquor in his room," I said. "Search it. He's got spray paint cans in his room. Search it. Eric's fucked up, and you need to know about it. I'm getting out of here before he gets back, because I'm not gonna deal with him right now."

Mrs. Harris wanted me to stay, to sit down and talk with Eric about this, as if we were in the school counselor's office or something. I shook my head. "I'm gone," I said as I got back in the car to go home.

As it turned out, Trevor had gone on his own mission of sorts. When I went to the Harrises' house, he drove back to the bus stop, where Eric and his friends had all left their backpacks while they continued their snowball fight. Trevor pulled up, grabbed Eric's bag, threw it in his car, and took off back to my house.

My mom decided that we were going to confront Eric. Once I got home, the three of us got in her car; my mom was driving, I was in the passenger seat, and Trevor sat in the back.

We drove back down the street to the bus stop. As we pulled up, my mom rolled down her window and called for Eric to come over.

"I said to the kids, 'Lock the doors. I'm just going to unroll the window a crack,' Judy Brown recalled. "And they did, and I said, 'Eric, I've got your backpack and I'm taking it over to your mom's. Meet us over there."

Eric's response shocked all three of them. His face turned bright red, and suddenly he began shrieking and pounding on the car, pulling as hard as he could on the door handle. He screamed at them to let him in.

No one, not even Brooks, had seen Eric act like this before.

"He just went crazy," Judy Brown said. "I started to pull away slowly, and he wouldn't let go. I said, 'Back away from the car. We'll meet you at your mom's.' He didn't listen. He just kept screaming, 'Give me my backpack!' Trevor moved over to the other side of the car, away from him. We were all scared."

Judy drove to Eric's house; Kathy Harris was standing in the driveway. Judy got out of the car and gave the backpack to her, explaining what had happened to Brooks's windshield.

"Normally a kid throwing a snowball at a car wouldn't upset me that much," Judy said. "I understand that kids can get carried away. But because we had heard he was going to do something to vandalize Brooks's car, it made me think this was on purpose."

Kathy Harris's eyes began to well up with tears. Judy immediately became sympathetic. She remembers Kathy Harris as being "very sweet, a very nice lady."

*At the time, Judy didn't think much of Eric's bag; she had no idea that
Eric was already building pipe bombs at that time, or that his journal contained entries about how much he hated school.*

"To this day, I wonder what might have been in that bag," she says.

*Later that evening, Kathy Harris called Judy at home to discuss the
matter further. According to Judy, Kathy wanted to listen, but her husband, Wayne, kept saying that Eric didn't mean it.*

*"He said, 'This is just kids' stuff. The truth is, Eric's afraid of you.' I
said, 'Look, your son isn't afraid of me—he came after me at my car.' And
he said, 'My son said that he is afraid of you.' He didn't want to hear that
his son had done anything wrong."*

My mom told us about her phone call with the Harrises, and we sat
around talking about it in our living room. By now my dad was home
from work, so we brought him up to speed on the situation. I told my parents about the other things Eric had been doing, and Aaron backed me
up, because he knew about it as well.

I was still seething. It helped a little to know that my parents were on
my side, and that Eric's parents were dealing with him at the same
moment. Nonetheless, I felt so much anger that night. I was used to getting shit from the bullies. I didn't expect it from people I used to call my
friends.

The next day at school, I heard through my friends that Eric was still
angry. My friends didn't tell me specifics, but they said Eric was threatening me. I went home and told my mom, who called the police. An officer came to our house, and we talked to him at length about what was
going on.

My mom described the windshield incident. "He thinks he got away
with it," she told the officer. "Please, just go over there and let him know

that he didn't." The officer was sympathetic to the situation. He told us he understood how upsetting a bully could be. He said he would pay a visit to the Harris home, only a few blocks away, and have a chat with them in an effort to rattle Eric a little.

I'm guessing that he must have done just that, because later that night, we got another phone call from the Harrises. This time, it was Mr. Harris, letting us know that he was bringing Eric over to our house to apologize.

My mom took Aaron and me aside. "I want both of you in the back bedroom, and don't come out," she said. We went, and we listened at the door as Eric came in.

"Eric came over and stood in our doorway, and he just had this fake tone to his voice," Judy said. " 'Mrs. Brown, I didn't mean any harm, and you know I would never do anything to hurt Brooks ...' I let him finish, but I could see right through the act. And then I said, 'You know, Eric, you can pull the wool over your dad's eyes, but you can't pull the wool over my eyes.'

"That seemed to surprise him. He said, 'Are you calling me a liar?' I remember that specifically. And I said, 'Yes, I am. And if you ever come up our street, or if you ever do anything to Brooks again—if I ever even see you on our street again—I'm calling the police.' "

Eric was shocked by Judy's words. He didn't say anything further; he just turned and stormed out to his father, who was waiting in the car.

"I don't think anyone had ever confronted him like that before," Judy said. "I think he was amazed that I didn't just go, 'It's okay, Eric. Yes.' Maybe he had gotten away with it for so long, manipulating people that way, that he was stunned when it didn't work."

Eric hadn't counted on my mother's attitude. He couldn't believe what she'd said to him.

At least, that's what I heard from people around school, since Eric and I weren't speaking anymore.

Dylan tried to make peace between us, but he always failed. Eric wanted nothing to do with me, and after what had happened to my wind- shield, I felt the same way toward him. Dylan and I would still go out to have cigarettes together, and Eric would refuse to go along because I was there. Sometimes I would go visit Dylan while he was working at Blackjack Pizza, and then Eric would show up and I would have to leave. I wished I could do something to improve the situation. But if that meant talking to Eric again, I refused. I was too angry.

However, I had no idea that, in the privacy of his study, Eric was qui- etly plotting his revenge.

8

the web pages

IN MARCH OF 1998, I WAS WALKING TO CLASS WHEN DYLAN approached me with a small piece of paper. On it was written the address for a Web site.

"I think you should take a look at this tonight," Dylan said.

I shrugged. "Okay. Anything special?" I figured at the time that it was the address for some new program Dylan had uncovered.

"It's Eric's Web site," he said. "You need to see it. And you can't tell Eric I gave it to you."

I nodded. "All right."

That night I logged on for the first time. Sure enough, it was Eric's page; I recognized the more familiar features, like the "Jo Momma" joke section; all of us would sit around and tell those. "Jo Momma" jokes are a takeoff of the traditional momma joke, only they're made to be deliberately bad. The humor came from seeing just how lame you could make them. We'd say things like, "Jo Momma is so poor she lives in a two-story Dorito bag." "Jo Momma is so fat she uses a Greyhound bus for roller blades." "Jo Momma is so dumb that she has seven extra fingers and two extra toes and she still can't count to 29."

However, Eric had several pages that clearly were not meant as a joke. They were brutal, savage attacks on everything he hated about the world. One of them had to do with me. Eric had written:

My belief is that if I say something, it goes. I am the law, if you don't like it, you die. If I don't like you or I don't like what you want me to do, you die. If I do something incorrect, oh fucking well, you die. Dead people can't do many things like argue, whine, bitch, complain, narc, rat out, criticize, or even fucking talk. So that's the only way to solve arguments with all you fuckheads out there, I just kill! God I can't wait till I can kill you people. I'll just go to some downtown area in some big-ass city and blow up and shoot everything I can. Feel no remorse, no sense of shame. Ich sage FICT TU! I will rig up explosives all over a town and detonate each one of them at will after I mow down a whole fucking area full of you snotty ass rich mother fucking high strung godlike attitude having worthless piece of shit whores. I don't care if I live or die in the shootout, all I want to do is to kill and injure as many of you pricks as I can, especially a few people. Like Brooks Brown.

I sat there staring at the screen for a moment. It was unexpected, to say the least.

On another page, Eric had posted my phone number, along with a specific list of everything he hated about me. On yet another, he encouraged would-be killers to seek me out, and promised a reward for my head.

Eric had an entire three-page document dedicated to the building of pipe bombs. He gave specific instructions on what ingredients to use, along with updates on his own progress. He described the bombs he'd already built, and the successful detonation of one of them. The entry read:

Mother fucker blew BIG. Pazzie was a complete success and it blew dee fuck outa a little creek bed. Flipping thing was heart-

*pounding gut-wrenching brain-twitching ground-moving insane-
ly cool! His brothers haven't found a target yet though.*

*Atlanta, Phobus, Peltro, and Pazzie are complete, for those
of who [sic] that don't know what they are, they are the first 4
true pipe bombs created entirely from scratch by the rebels REB
and VoDkA. Atlanta and Phobus are each 1 1/4" by 6" pipes,
Peltro is 1" by 6", and Pazzie is 3/4" by 5". Each is packed with
powder that we got from fountains, mortar shells, and cracker-
ing balls. Each also has a 14" mortar shell type fuse. Now our
only problem is to find the place that will be "ground zero."*

Eric had posted detailed descriptions of the "Rebel Missions" he
and Dylan had carried out in the neighborhood. In this example, they set
off firecrackers outside the house of the person they had targeted for
the evening:

*Awwww yeya. This mission was so fuckin fun man. OK, first
of all, my dad was the only parent home, so it was much easier
getting out ... but still hard since all those rocks in my backyard
make so much noise ...*

*We watched as some lights in the Target's house went on,
then off. Maybe the bastard heard something. But when the (firecracker) strip started, he turned his bedroom lights off. The strip
lasted for about 30 seconds ... we think ... It was very fucking
long. Almost all of it went off, loud and bright. Everything worked
exactly how we wanted it to. After about 15 minutes we started
down the bike trail to the next target. The first target's lights were
on again in the bedroom, but we think we got away undetected.
While we were walking to the next target, we shot some stuff.
Heh, VoDkA brought his sawed off BB gun and a few BB's, too.*

So we loaded it, pumped it, and fired it off a few shots at some houses and trees and stuff. We probably didn't do any damage to any houses, but we aren't sure …

…Ok people, I'm gonna let you in on the big secret of our clan. We ain't no god damn stupid ass quake clan! We are more of a gang. We plan out and execute missions. Anyone pisses us off, we do a little deed to their house. Eggs, [TP], superglue, busyboxes, large amounts of fireworks, you name it and we will probably or already have done it. We have many enemies in our school, therefore we make many missions. It is sort of a night-time tradition for us.

Based on the Web site, however, it seemed clear that these "Rebel Missions" weren't going to satisfy Eric for much longer. Writing, "I live in Denver and would love to kill all its residents," Eric offered one final warning to his readers:

Well all you people out there can just kiss my ass and die. From now on, I don't give a fuck what almost any of you mutha fuckas have to say, unless I respect you which is highly unlikely, but for those of you who happen to know me and know that I respect you, may peace be with you and don't be in my line of fire. For the rest of you, you all better fucking hide in your house because im comin [sic] for EVERYONE soon, and I WILL be armed to the fuckin teeth and I WILL shoot to kill and I WILL fucking KILL EVERYTHING! No I am not crazy, crazy is just a word, to me it has no meaning, everyone is different, but most of you fuckheads out there in society, going to your everyday fucking jobs and doing your everyday routine shitty things, I say fuck you and die. If you got a problem with my thoughts, come tell me and I'll kill you, because ... god damnit, DEAD PEOPLE DON'T ARGUE!

I'd seen enough. I told my parents.

"This was not a little kid's joke," said Randy Brown of Eric Harris's Web pages. "Threats against everybody, wanting to kill everybody, the violence of it all. And then there was his specific threat against Brooks. I didn't know anything about threat assessment at the time—we'd never even heard the words before—but those are certainly signs that we know now of serious threats."

Brooks and his parents got into a heated argument over what to do next. Randy wanted to go to the Harrises and tell them. He suggested faxing the pages to Mr. Harris anonymously. But Judy Brown objected. She said Mr. Harris had done nothing about the windshield incident; he hadn't even offered to pay for the damage.

The family eventually agreed to call the police. That night, Deputy Miller of the Jefferson County Sheriff's Department came to the Brown home to look at the pages for himself. It was March 18, 1998.

Randy Brown handed over printed copies of the Web pages to Miller, and explained his family's past troubles with Eric. They discussed the pipe bombs and Eric's desire to kill more people. Most of all, Randy expressed his concern for Brooks's safety.

Judy and Randy gave Dylan Klebold's name to Miller as well, because he and Eric were such close friends—and Dylan had been mentioned on the site as being part of the "Rebel Missions." However, Brooks had not told his parents that Dylan was the one who gave him the Web site address in the first place.

I never told my parents that I got the address from Dylan until after the shootings. I was worried that if I did, Eric would find out, and then Dylan would be in trouble with him for having warned me. I simply told my parents that a friend had given it to me, and that if Eric ever found out who, he would hurt him.

In truth, I don't know what Dylan's motives were for giving me that Web site. Maybe he was trying to warn me. Maybe he thought the site was funny, and just didn't take it as seriously as I did.

Or maybe Eric did want him to give the address to me. Maybe Dylan was in on it, and both of them wanted to send me a scare. I didn't know.

I have no doubt that Dylan knew exactly what was on that Web site when he gave me the address. He might not have been posting things on it himself, but at the very least, Eric was keeping him up to speed. So I was afraid to go back to him and mention it.

I was afraid to call the police at first, too. In my dealings at Columbine, I had learned that if you report someone, nothing gets done—and then the person finds out who reported him and makes that person's life that much worse. At Columbine, if you got into a fight with someone and you were scared of him, you might mention this to the administration; the administration would then bring both of you into a "counseling session" to try to work things out. That didn't work. So I feared calling the police, but at the same time, I knew something needed to be done.

My parents did their best to explain to the officer about the Web pages, the references to *Doom*, and other computer terms. The officer admitted that he knew little about computers, but told us that there were others at the station who would understand better.

The officer seemed very sympathetic to me. He could tell that the whole situation had really freaked me out, and he told me a little about his own experiences with bullies in an effort to make me feel better. He also promised us that the situation would be investigated further.

A week or so later, my parents phoned the police station to follow up on their complaint. They made an appointment to see Detective John Hicks on March 31.

"We actually went over there twice," Judy Brown said. "They couldn't find the Web pages the first time, so we printed out new copies and went a second time. The minute he saw them, he said, 'I have only seen one or two like this. This is serious.' His demeanor immediately changed when he started to read it."

According to the Browns, Detective Hicks brought in two members of the bomb squad to explain to the Browns how to spot a pipe bomb. He also asked the bomb squad to check if there had been any reports of bombs being set off in the area. When they looked into it, the answer was that yes, there was activity.

The Browns say Detective Hicks warned them that there might not be enough in the pages to legally accuse Eric of a threat against Brooks. The wording read, "I want to kill and maim … especially a few people … LIKE Brooks Brown."

"He wasn't sure if that wording was going to be good enough to go for everything," Randy explained. "But he added, 'I've certainly got him for the pipe bomb building and the detonating.' So we knew they had him for at least something. There was no point during that meeting that we didn't think they were going to get this kid.

"That's why it was such a shock when the attack on Columbine happened, and we found out that nothing had been done."

A few days after my parents went to see the police, the word around school was that Eric and Dylan had gotten in big trouble over something. No one knew what it was; Eric and Dylan wouldn't talk about it. But we heard that both of them were in counseling.

I came home and told my parents. My dad had a big look of relief on his face. "That's it," he said. "They did their job."

My mom asked me if I could find out what specifically they were in trouble for, and I said there was no way; they were keeping it quiet.

"But Mom, it's big," I said. "Everybody is talking about it."

It only made sense to think that the counseling was for the pipe bomb building and the hate, and everything else that was on Eric's Web site.

What the Browns didn't know was that in reality, Eric and Dylan had just experienced their day in court for a van break-in that had happened at the end of January.

On January 30, 1998, Eric and Dylan were hanging out together in a parking lot near Deer Creek Canyon Road. They were parked next to a van loaded with various pieces of electrical equipment.

At first, Eric and Dylan were just killing time, breaking bottles and lighting a few small fireworks. Yet their attention was drawn to the van. When they realized that no one was around, they decided to force their way into it. While Eric kept watch from inside his car, Dylan smashed in the van's window with a rock and began unloading equipment.

Once they had filled up the back seat of Eric's new Honda Prelude— Eric's parents had given him a car now that he finally had his driver's license—the two took off and pulled over a few miles away to check out what they had stolen.

Officer Tim Walsh of the Jefferson County Sheriff's Office was on routine patrol in the area. He noticed the two boys and parked his car a short distance away to observe them. After about five minutes, he approached, shone a flashlight into Eric's face, and asked him what they were doing.

At first, Eric and Dylan claimed they had found the equipment stacked up on the side of the road. When Walsh made it clear that he didn't believe that story, they cracked. The boys admitted what they had done, and Walsh took them into custody.

Their parents were furious. Eric and Dylan received significant grounding as punishment. However, both of their fathers backed them up when they appeared before Jefferson County Magistrate John DeVita in early April of 1998.

"This has been a rather traumatic experience, and I think it's probably good ... that they got caught the first time," Tom Klebold told DeVita.

Eric and Dylan were sentenced to one year in a juvenile diversion program, where they would be forced to undergo four days of classes dealing with anger management and drunk driving, 45 hours of community service, multiple fines, and counseling. They received this sentence the same week that the Browns met with Detective Hicks at the Jefferson County Sheriff's Office.

According to the Browns, when Detective Hicks ran a search for prior offenses on Eric Harris, the report of the break-in came up. However, the Browns did not learn that Dylan had been involved in the break-in as well. So when Brooks came home and said that both Eric and Dylan were in trouble, they had no reason to suspect anything other than the Web pages.

As for Eric, he offered two completely different perspectives on the incident. In a school essay he wrote on November 18, 1998, he described the incident to his teacher:

After a very unique experience in a real live police station being a real live criminal, I had lots of time to think about what I did.... As I waited, I cried, I hurt, and I felt like hell … My parents lost all respect and trust in me and I am still slowly regaining it. That experience showed me that no matter what crime you think of committing, you will get caught, that you must, absolutely must, think things through before you act, and that just because you can do something doesn't mean you should. To this day I still do not have a hard realistic reason why we broke into that car, but since we did, we have been set on a track that makes it mandatory for me to be a literal angel until March of '99.

However, in his own personal journal, which was obtained by members of the media in late 2001, Eric described the incident much, much differently:

Isn't America supposed to be the land of the free? How come if I'm free, I can't deprive a stupid fucking dumbshit from his possessions if he leaves them sitting in the front seat of his fucking van out in plain sight and in the middle of fucking nowhere on a Fri-fucking-day night? NATURAL SELECTION. Fucker should be shot.

Just as he had done with Judy Brown several months earlier, Eric Harris was saying one thing and thinking another. The diversion program would not stop Eric's hatred—nor would it stop him from secretly beginning a plot with Dylan Klebold to attack Columbine High School.

Our whole family was on edge for some time after we discovered Eric's Web pages. We kept a baseball bat by the door, in case Eric tried to break into our house. If we saw a car drive by slowly or heard people making noise outside, my brother and I would sneak out with my dad and hide behind the bushes, watching. My dad installed brighter lights for the front and rear doors, as well as a motion-detector light.

We lived like that for a long time.

Things would still happen. On April 11, 1998, I received a short e-mail from an unknown sender. It said something like, "I know you're an enemy of Eric's. I know where you live and what car you drive." We reported it to the police, but unfortunately the e-mail was accidentally erased before we could give them a copy.

One time my dad opened the front door in time to see a chain of fire-crackers going off on our porch. Obviously, there was no way to prove who had done this, either, but when you read Eric's descriptions of his "Rebel Missions," it seems pretty obvious.

On another night, we were sitting in the living room at about 11:30 when Aaron suddenly looked up and said, "Did you hear that? I heard some glass breaking or something." We went outside and looked around, but we didn't see anything.

The next morning, my dad went out to the garage and noticed that his car had tiny red dots all over it. So did half the garage. Then we looked at the windows on the garage door, and there was a little hole in one of them, barely an inch in diameter. Someone had shot a paintball through the window.

The police came and looked at the car, but obviously there was no way to prove who was responsible. However, my parents and I got into the car and drove up and down the neighborhood. We saw that a lot of houses had been shot with paintballs. The path traced right back up to Eric's street.

During this time, I stopped talking to Dylan altogether. I didn't know what to trust him with anymore. I was freaked out about the Web pages, and he was good friends with Eric, so I avoided him.

One thing that concerned me was that after a few months went by, Eric's Web site hadn't been taken down. There were things on the pages that had been changed, but nonetheless, Eric was still posting angry rants. My parents tried to get in touch with Detective Hicks, to see how the investigation had progressed. They were never able to reach him.

In a CBS 60 Minutes II *investigation two years after the assault on Columbine, it was learned that a search warrant had been drafted for Eric Harris's home. However, the warrant was never presented to a judge. Had it been served, the police would have found pipe bombs, gunpowder, Eric's angry journal rants—and perhaps early evidence of a plot he and Dylan were already beginning to hatch.*

Even before they were arrested for breaking into the van in January, Eric and Dylan felt like the whole world was against them. Some have theorized that the trauma of this incident reinforced their feelings of persecution, cementing their bond and making them hungry for revenge.

Eric's journal indicates that sometime in their junior year they devised their plan to attack Columbine High School. Police reports show that in the spring of 1998, Dylan wrote in Eric's yearbook about "killing enemies, blowing stuff up, killing cops! My wrath for January's incident will be godlike. Not to mention our revenge in the commons" (the Columbine High School cafeteria, where Eric and Dylan had suffered at the hands of bullies since freshman year).

Eric wrote in Dylan's yearbook, "God I can't wait until they die. I can taste the blood now ... You know what I hate? MANKIND! Kill everything ... kill everything ..."

In a journal entry that was not released until nearly three years after the massacre, the Browns discovered just how seriously Eric had plotted against them—and, twelve months before the shootings, against the school. The entry was dated April 26, 1998:

Sometime in April me and V will get revenge and kick natural selection up a few notches ... We will be in all black. Dusters, black Army pants, and we will get custom shirts that say R or V in the background in one big letter and NBK *[Eric's nickname for the planned attack, named for the film* Natural Born Killers*]* in the front in a smaller font ...

First we will go to the house of ... Brooks in the morning before school starts and before anyone is even awake. We go in, we silently kill each inhabitant and then pin down Brooks ... Then take our sweet time pissing on them, spitting on them and just torturing the hell out of them. Once we are done we set time bombs to burn the houses down and take any weaponry we find, who knows me [sic] may get lucky. Then get totally prepared and during A lunch we go and park in our spots. With sunglasses on we start carrying in all our bags of terrorism and anarchism shit into our table. Being very casual and silent about it, it's all for a science/band/English project or something ...

Once the first wave starts to go off and the chaos begins, V opens fire and I start lobbin' the firebombs. Then I open fire, V starts lobbin' more crickets. Then if we can go upstairs and go to each classroom we can pick off fuckers at our will. If we still can we will hijack some awesome car, and drive off to the neighborhood of our choice and start torching houses with Molotov cocktails. By that time cops will be all over us and we start to kill them too! We use bombs, fire bombs and anything we fucking can to

kill and damage as much as we fucking can … I want to leave a
lasting impression on the world.

The plan was in place, and no one knew. Not me, not my parents, not
the school. The police could have stopped it, had they acted on my family's report. But they didn't.

The warning signs were there. The threats, Eric's Web pages, the
"Rebel Missions" in the neighborhood. Today, they're all painfully obvious. But back then, no one was putting them together. Not even me. In
the back of my mind, I couldn't imagine why a person would murder anyone else, not even a person who wrote the kinds of things that Eric did.

The following summer, I moved on with my life. I believed the danger
had passed.

9

suburban life

BY THE END OF MY JUNIOR YEAR, SCHOOL SHOOTINGS WERE MAKING their way into the news.

The first one I heard about was in 1997, when Luke Woodham killed two students and wounded seven others in Pearl, Mississippi. Two months later, in West Paducah, Kentucky, Michael Carneal killed three students at a high school prayer service. In March of 1998, Mitchell Johnson and Andrew Golden of Jonesboro, Arkansas—one aged thirteen, the other eleven—set off a fire alarm to make their fellow students run outside, then opened fire from the trees. They killed four students and a teacher. Finally, Kip Kinkel went on a rampage In Springfield, Oregon in May of 1998. He murdered both of his parents at home, then went to school, killed two students, and wounded twenty-two others.

Each of these stories made national headlines; the attacks on Paducah and Jonesboro happened right in the middle of my junior year. In fact, I read a great deal about them during debate class. We would hold "extemporane-ous meetings" where we went through media clippings from the past week and discussed them, and the shootings came up several times.

Violence had plagued inner-city schools for some time, but these shootings marked its first real appearance in primarily white, middle- to upper-middle-class suburbs. And to me, it seemed the location wasn't the only unusual thing about these shootIngs. In the past, when a kid shot somebody at school, it was because he had it in for the victim and had come looking for him or her. Now the motives seemed different. Now we were seeing people go into schools and whip out a gun for no other reason than to randomly wipe out as many people as possible.

When we talked in class about the shootings, kids would make jokes about how "it was going to happen at Columbine next." They would say that Columbine was absolutely primed for it, because of the bullying and the hate that were so prevalent at our school.

Columbine had already seen its own tragedy that year. In 1998, a student named Robert Craig had killed his father and then himself with a gun at their home.

The students' response varied. Some kids didn't give a shit. Their basic attitude was, "Aw, great, another death-metal guy died. Whoop-whoop." However, friends of mine who had been close to Robert became very upset. The people who weren't in the popular crowd went through a hell of a time when Robert died; seeing the jocks laughing about it made things even worse.

I had talked to Robert Craig a couple of times. I wasn't close to him or anything, but we had a few of the same friends. He seemed like a good kid, and it upset me a lot when I heard the news; I wrote a poem about it in one of my notebooks, trying to make sense of the whole thing. The violence had seemed to come out of nowhere; Robert had acted depressed sometimes, but plenty of people at Columbine acted depressed. It wasn't something that we thought would end with murdering your dad and then killing yourself.

Still, I didn't dwell on Robert's death for long. Nor did I dwell on my problems with Eric. I spent the summer between junior and senior year playing in a band with a few friends and my little brother. I played drums, Aaron was on keyboards, and my friends Doug and Kevin handled vocals, guitar, and trumpet. We called ourselves "Second Sedition." The way we saw it, the first sedition had been in 1776. We were the second one. I wrote a good deal of our lyrics, and Aaron was an absolute master when it came to music.

We recorded a demo CD and sent it out in the hopes of landing a few live gigs around the Denver area. We couldn't make it happen. We did play with a few other bands in Clement Park at the end of our junior year, but we couldn't land any bar gigs. We were told that our sound was "too dark." To us, that was a compliment, but it didn't exactly help us build up an audience. The band pretty much fell apart by the beginning of senior year, but such is life. It had been fun.

That fall, I picked up again with drama and debate. My favorite high school memories center around our speech contests. Sometimes we would travel for competitions, and have to stay in dorm rooms or something similar overnight. We would pull all sorts of crazy antics when we were on the road.

Nick Baumgart, as always, kept us laughing. One time we were hanging out in our rooms during a competition. There were two beds in the room, and a couple of guys were jumping from one bed to the other, trying to do tricks in mid-air. Nick, not wanting to be outdone, got in on the action. "I'm going to do it," he said, "and not only that, I'm going to do a somersault!"

So Nick took a flying leap and started spinning. Unfortunately for him, he was a little too enthusiastic, and he hit the ceiling. With his face. It was one of those stucco ceilings, with all of the little points and rough edges; this little shower of tiny stucco pieces came down, and so did Nick. His face looked kind of interesting for a while after that.

Debate competition was becoming better for me each year. My skills were improving, I liked the people I was working with, and by senior year, I was ready to make a run at Nationals. Seniors pair up with freshmen in the debate program each year, to mentor them; I mentored a new kid in the program named Daniel Mauser. He was a smart kid, and I liked him immediately, so I told him what I could.

In theatre, too, I felt at home. The first play of our senior year was *Frankenstein*, and I won the role of Frankenstein's monster. The play *Frankenstein* isn't anything like the old Boris Karloff movie, with the giant mumbling monster who lurches around with corks coming out of his neck. The stage version of *Frankenstein* is much more loyal to the book's theme of society fearing what it doesn't understand. Frankenstein's monster is a deep, troubled creature who was created by a scientist, then dismissed as an abomination. From there, he wanders alone, labeled as a "freak" by the rest of society and rejected by everyone who sees him. The cruelty eventually leads the monster to seek revenge.

I dove into that role with enthusiasm.

Dylan got himself onto the sound crew for *Frankenstein*. It was the first time I'd really spent any time with him since he'd pointed me toward Eric's Web pages. I had calmed down over the whole mess during the summer, but I still wasn't talking to Dylan until the first day of *Frankenstein* rehearsals in September.

That day, the ice between us broke. We didn't ever mention Eric's Web site; we just started talking again, as if we had silently accepted that the past was the past. That night we went out for coffee at the nearby Perkins.

There were a few things about Dylan that had changed. He'd grown his hair out a lot longer, and he had much more of a "grunge" look to his clothing. Beyond his physical appearance, though, he seemed like the same old Dylan.

He and I started hanging out again during those weeks of play rehearsal. It became a habit to grab a soda or a coffee somewhere and just sit down and talk about things. Sometimes we talked about school. Other times we talked about music. Dylan would tell me about how great

Rammstein and KMFDM were, and I'd fire back with a spirited defense of Insane Clown Posse. Dylan was into very dark, fuck-the-world kinds of music. It wasn't my thing, but we had some great conversations regardless.

Dylan told me he was thinking about applying to the University of Arizona to study computer design. He sounded like he was making plans for his future. I encouraged him.

One time we spent the whole night reminiscing about the old video games we used to play. We laughed about the first time we'd played *Mortal Kombat* in front of our moms. Dylan recalled that *Ninja Gaiden* was the very first Nintendo game we'd ever played together back in grade school.

We loved talking about old times. We knew we would never again be as close as we'd been in those grade school days; he and I were different people now, with our own interests and groups of friends. Still, we had a long history with each other, and those nights after rehearsal—sitting at Perkins with a cigarette and a couple of Cokes, talking about the way things used to be—made for great times.

The seniors in our theatre troupe decided to produce a special video for *Frankenstein*. Not only was it a farewell project for the drama students, it was a farewell to Mrs. Caruthers, who had been one of our favorite teachers over the past four years.

For the first part of the tape, we did interviews with the cast and crew about their favorite memories of Mrs. Caruthers. We then added in footage from rehearsal, along with scenes from the movie *Young Frankenstein*.

Dylan, Zach Heckler and I were the three people who did "commentary" for the tape.

The three of us sat down in the front row of the Columbine auditorium and set the camera down on the stage. Our job was to review all of the people in the *Frankenstein* program and offer both compliments and "inside jokes" that only those involved in the department would understand. Later we would intercut this footage with scenes from *Young Frankenstein* and show the finished version to other people in the drama club.

It was a lot of fun to make, and the camera caught a few moments of Dylan coming out of his quiet shell. We went backwards through the program, reading each name and offering a few observations. The first name Zach read off was Principal DeAngelis.

Dylan leaned in toward the camera. "Ha ha ha," he said.

The three of us roasted each other as much as we could. Dylan, who had sat quietly through some of the early jokes, happily came out of his shell for some ribbing on me.

Dylan gave special mention to the makeup crew. "Damn good job," he said. "Brooks, you were ugly as shit. And that's hard to beat, with the way you look normally."

"I was uglier than I even am usually," I agreed.

"Don't get fire within twenty feet of the pants," Dylan warned, referring to my "Frankenstein monster" costume. "There were about thirty different chemicals put into that." (This was true, actually. Dylan and I made the pants using an old pair of jeans that we soaked in gasoline and paint thinner to make them look as horrible as possible. After the final performance, we took them out to a field and flicked a cigarette at them. They immediately burst into flames.)

"Zach, how did this guy do on sound?" I asked, referring to Dylan.

"Oh, he sucked," Zach replied.

Dylan threw his hands up. "Thank you!"

"And everybody was crying about it, because it was late," Zach added. Dylan hadn't finished preparing the sound cues by Mrs. C's original deadline.

"Yeah, yeah," Dylan said. "I'd like to bring forth attention to this, actually—for three years now, I've been doing this job. Just a guess here, but I think I know what I'm doing—"

"Okay, shut up," I said. We all laughed.

That was how the video went. We picked out names, made a few good-natured jokes, then complimented the person and moved on. We had especially kind words for Mrs. Caruthers, whom all three of us were going to miss.

"You're losing your entire sound and light crew," I said to the camera. "This will be the last play we get to do with you."

The three of us asked for bribes in exchange for passing along our knowledge to the next crop of students. "Hey, Mrs. C, next Saturday—big ol' party," Dylan said. "Heineken, Miller … We need you." It was a running joke for theatre students to try and get Mrs. Caruthers to buy booze for us, because we knew she never would.

We offered our thanks to Mrs. Caruthers for her inspiration. "From the people who have been working with you the longest, we want to say, very beautiful job with all the plays," I said.

"Very well done," Dylan added. "All of these kids over the years—I don't know how, but … you put the whole thing together."

"You've taught us how to work on our own," I said. "We really did this play on our own, and it was fantastic. And we owe it to you, Mrs. C."

After the final performance that night, everyone from the show watched the video. My mom took pictures. There was Dylan, laughing and having a good time. Just like everyone else.

Throughout all of this, I was still avoiding Eric Harris. And Eric was avoiding me.

It was hard for Dylan. He didn't talk much about it, but you could tell. Nobody wants to be in the position of being friends with two people who hate each other.

I figured it wouldn't be for much longer, though. By December, we were signing up for spring term of senior year. Only one more semester to go; then Dylan would be off to college, and I would be off to do whatever the heck I decided to do, and we would be free of Columbine forever. Worries about Eric Harris were the farthest thing from my mind.

10

friendship renewed

IN OUR FINAL SEMESTER AT COLUMBINE HIGH SCHOOL, I STARTED talking to Eric Harris again.

It was the first day of spring term. First period, I had gym. In second period, I would be working as a student assistant to Mrs. Caruthers, grading tests and assisting with miscellaneous projects. The first two hours of the day were pretty uneventful; just your standard first-day-of-school orientation kind of thing. Then I walked into third-hour philosophy.

At first, everything seemed great. I was really excited about that class. Mr. Kritzer was one of my favorite teachers, and this was the first time that a philosophy class would be offered at Columbine. The first person I saw when I walked in the room was Becca Heins, who I knew was an absolute riot to be around. I was sitting next to her, so we started talking as the rest of the students filed in.

Then I looked over my shoulder. Eric was sitting behind me.

That was a shock, to say the least. In all four years at Columbine, I don't think Eric and I had ever shared a class. Yet here he was. We hadn't spoken since the windshield incident nearly a year ago, and the moment I saw him, I felt all that old tension returning. It was very uneasy for both of us. We went through third period not saying a word to each other.

After the period was over, I headed for fourth-hour Creative Writing class. Lo and behold, there was Eric again—and this time, Dylan was there, too. So this was going to be even more interesting. Becca was in this class, too, and so was Nate Dykeman. They all sat together, but I sat on the other side of the room, kind of cursing to myself.

Three and a half years of no classes with Eric Harris, and now, when I know the guy hates me, we have two classes in a row. Unbelievable. I spent that night thinking it over. I knew there was no way I could go through four months of this.

I decided, "Fuck this. I'm not going to have someone sitting behind me where I'm worried that he's going to be stabbing me in the back or giving me shit. I'm not going to sit in fourth hour and ignore all my friends because Eric's with them. I have to make up with him."

Obviously, I was still angry about what had happened the year before. But a lot of time had passed, and that initial rage had dulled. Besides, my mind was weighing the benefits of making peace against the difficulty of the next four months if I didn't.

The next morning, I had a cigarette before class, to prepare. Then I walked into third hour just before the bell rang. Eric was already there.

I told Eric I wanted to bury the hatchet. I said we'd been pissed off at each other for long enough. I told him that I had changed a lot since last year, that I knew I had been a piece of shit in a lot of ways, and that I hoped he felt the same way about himself. "We were both immature," I said. "I just want to move on."

Eric seemed surprised. I don't think he ever expected that I would extend an olive branch, much less admit I had been a jerk. He shrugged and said, "Cool."

It was strange. By the time class started, we were joking about what stupid little kids we had both been. Eric said there were probably two sophomores out there doing the same sort of thing right now, and that they wouldn't be talking again until senior year, either. It was funny. We laughed.

If someone had told me the year before that I would ever share a laugh with Eric Harris again, I would have called him or her insane. Yet here we were. And once fourth hour rolled around, I moved over and sat next to him, Dylan, and Becca.

Dylan was stunned at the turn of events. He and I went out for a cigarette that day, and Eric was with us. We told Dylan that things were cool between us. To be honest, I think Dylan was one reason why Eric and I patched things up so easily. Both of us knew the strain our rift had put on him; nobody likes to play the go-between.

Several people have suggested to me that Eric found excuses to hate me back in junior year because he felt I was threatening his friendship with Dylan. After all, he had pushed away their other friends one by one. The theory makes sense. When you're younger, and you live in a society like Columbine, you get the feeling that friendship is finite and can be tossed away easily, that starting a friendship with one person means losing friendships with others. Yet you learn through experience that friendship can be infinite.

Eric came from a background of constantly moving around with his family; who knows how many friendships were cut off for him each time? In Dylan, he saw a best friend, and he feared anything that could take that away. From there, he found excuses to make me a target.

I was hoping all of that would be behind us now.

I know it seems strange that I would make peace with someone who had threatened to kill me, vandalized my parents' house, and refused to speak to me for the past year. However, it just made sense to create peace. I wasn't looking to become Eric's best friend, but I wanted to be able to hang out with Dylan without it being an issue. I wanted to be able to go to class and not worry about Eric. When he and I had mutual friends and shared classes, it just made sense.

People do have the potential to change. It had been over a year since we'd had our problems. I figured that if Eric turned out to be as big a prick as he'd been before, I would stop talking to him. However, if he had grown up, then why not give him the chance to prove it?

The first thing I noticed about Eric was that he didn't get angry nearly as easily anymore. Things that used to set off his temper would just make him chuckle now. He seemed calm, composed. As strange as this sounds today, he seemed a lot less prone to violence.

This was especially impressive since, as always, the jocks were still targeting him and Dylan. Soon after we'd made peace, I was smoking cigarettes with them when a bunch of football players drove by, yelled something, and threw a glass bottle that shattered near Dylan's feet. I was pissed, but Eric and Dylan didn't even flinch. "Don't worry about it, man," Dylan said. "It happens all the time."

Another time, Eric and Dylan were searched for drugs after someone in school "reported them" as a way to harass them. Eric and Dylan were removed from class and searched. Their lockers and their cars were searched as well. No drugs were turned up, but the two of them had been humiliated nonetheless.

They shrugged it off.

Eric didn't seem to be as quiet in front of people as he'd once been. At one point in Creative Writing, we had to do a "personification essay," describing what it would feel like to be a certain inanimate object. For example, you could write about what it feels like to be a desk, or a chair.

The assignment seemed ludicrous, and no one wanted to do it. So Eric decided to get crazy with it, by writing an essay about a shotgun and a shotgun shell getting married. The story ended with the two of them going off and having a bunch of little "pellet babies." It was one of the funniest damned things in the world, and when Eric read it in front of the class, everyone was cracking up.

I couldn't imagine anything like that happening in sophomore year. I couldn't imagine Eric getting up in front of the entire class and not only reading his work, but putting on such a "performance" that people would be rolling on the floor.

It seemed like Eric had found a new voice with his writing. We were assigned to write poetry, essays, and short stories, some fiction and some nonfiction. I saw a new side of Eric emerge through his writing on more than one occasion.

Eric wrote an essay about his childhood, in which he described playing "war" with his brother and a neighborhood girl at his old place in Michigan. He wrote about the joy and innocence of those early days, playing cops and robbers in the fields or hiding in the forest behind his house.

The teacher asked Eric to read it out loud in front of the class. He declined, but when I offered to read it for him, he said, "Sure," and handed it to me. I was glad to do it. It was a simple, pleasant story, authored by someone who seemed to have worked through many of his issues.

New sides of Dylan's personality came out in Mrs. Kelly's class, too. At one point we were given a "collaborative story" writing exercise. The idea was that one person would write the first paragraph of a story, then hand the paper to someone else, who would read it and then add on. I wound up collaborating with Dylan.

Earlier, we had been assigned to read a book called *A Prayer For Owen Meany*, by John Irving. It's supposed to be loaded with symbolism, but my friends and I didn't get into it. We disliked Owen Meany, who was supposed to be the hero. We also objected to the religious themes of the book, and resented the fact that we were being forced to read it for class.

I was in a sarcastic mood that day, so for the story's first paragraph, I wrote:

There is a fiery inferno surrounding you. Satan is sitting on his throne, pointing and laughing at you. A copy of A Prayer For Owen Meany *sits in front of you, next to a box full of the book. A sign has been placed next to the book that says, "Read all of these."*

Dylan could see where I was going, so when it came his turn to write, he added:

Just then, the god of coolness came down upon Satan. "Satan, this punishment is too cruel for any soul. What happened to fire and brimstone?" "Owen Meany is far worse, ha ha ha," replied Satan. Then the coolness god perished all copies of the book, saying that no soul deserved to read the tortuous, morbid, evil book. Then Hell was a happy place, and Satan started a chain of day-care centers.

Eric and Dylan were both making me laugh. They were fun to be around in those final months. We were friends just like before—only this time, the anger that had hung over them in junior year seemed to have dissipated and been replaced with wisecracks and an eagerness to finish up with school so they could move on with life. It was a welcome change—or so I felt.

There were days when we'd all ditch class together. One time I went with Eric, Dylan, and Becca to pick up sandwiches and eat them over at Eric's house. I hadn't been over there in a long time, and it felt strange to be there, but by now I felt at ease enough with Eric to not think twice about it. His parents weren't home at the time, which was probably a good thing. That would have been an awkward reunion, to say the least.

I didn't say anything to my parents about Eric at first. For the first month or so, I wasn't really sure if we would become friends again. We might have made peace, but I didn't know whether or not he had changed. That's the philosophy I go by: "Trust your neighbors, but lock your doors." I was being careful. Eric was being a good kid again? Go with it, I told myself. But don't get screwed over a second time.

However, by March I realized that things were going to be okay. I decided my parents should know that he and I had resolved our differences.

It didn't go well.

We were sitting at the dinner table, talking about school, and I just decided to bring up the subject.

"Well, you're not going to believe who I've made up with," I said.

Somehow my mom knew exactly who I meant. "Don't say it," she replied.

"It's Eric," I said. I laughed over how bizarre it was, expecting that my parents would laugh too.

They didn't. Instead, my mom stared at me, stone-faced.

"It's a trick," she said.

"I knew who Brooks meant the moment he said that I wouldn't believe it," Judy Brown said. *"Eric was the only kid who would have shocked me like that. So Brooks was right—I couldn't believe it. And one of the first things I said was, 'Don't trust him.' "*

Randy Brown reacted angrily. He remembers asking Brooks, "What the hell are you doing? This kid wanted to kill you!" He and Judy began a heated argument with their son, who they felt was ignoring common sense in making up with Eric.

Brooks was angry, because his parents seemed to be contradicting their own advice. He pointed out to both of them that they had taught him from an early age to give people a second chance if it seemed like they had changed.

"That was difficult, because we had always taught him that," Randy Brown recalls. "Because that's the same chance that Brooks never got from the other kids at Columbine. Once kids make up their mind that someone's not wanted, it's hard to break that down. But at the same time, Judy and I hadn't forgotten last year. We wanted Brooks to stay away from that kid."

The argument grew so intense that Brooks wound up storming out of the house. He drove to the nearby Perkins restaurant to get a cup of coffee and cool off.

My parents and I were still fighting all the time, even in senior year. We had a strange relationship, because I loved them so much and we talked about things that a lot of kids would never talk to their parents about. Yet when we fought, it would get very ugly and very personal. I made a lot of trips out to Perkins—sometimes with friends, other times by myself, but almost always to get out of the house for a while. I can't say we had a love/hate relationship, because I've never hated my parents. But it was certainly a rocky one.

That night, I was angry because my parents wouldn't trust my judgment. It was as if they thought I had forgotten everything that had happened the year before. I hadn't. How could anyone forget that? What I wanted them to understand was that I remembered the same things they did, yet I'd found it in my heart to get past it and start over. If I could do that, and I was the one most directly affected by Eric, I thought they should trust my decision. Especially with all of their lessons about giving people a second chance.

I did give some thought to what they'd said. I wondered if maybe I had allowed myself to forget things because it was convenient to do so. Nonetheless, I was determined to give Eric that second chance. I had made a lot of mistakes in my own life at that point, so I knew that to refuse someone a second chance when he's truly changed is really hurtful and demeaning.

What I didn't know was that my mom was right. Eric was putting on an act, and not just for me. He and Dylan weren't laughing at their troubles in class because they had grown up and learned to deal with them. They were laughing because they knew that, in only a few more months, they were going to shock everyone with their revenge.

11

the calm before the storm

THE COLUMBINE HIGH SCHOOL CLASS OF 1999 HAD ITS PICTURE TAKEN on the bleachers of the gymnasium, with close to four hundred kids packed together like one big, happy family. Up in the far left-hand corner of that picture were Eric, Dylan, and me.

Zach Heckler and Robyn Anderson were up there with us. We learned we would be doing two different poses: an "official" or serious class photo and a silly one. Since he was offering us the chance to do a "silly" picture, the photographer figured we wouldn't do anything to screw up the serious one. We were instructed to hold still for the extended exposure of the picture, so all of us gave our best "serious looks" to the camera.

When it came time for the "silly shot," Eric donned his KMFDM hat, and he and Dylan both put on shades. Eric suggested that, since we were having a camera pointed at us, it would be cool to point imaginary guns back. So the five of us pantomimed doing exactly that.

It seemed like a funny thing to do. I never thought twice about it.

People always ask about warning signs Eric and Dylan might have shown in the weeks before Columbine. By then, however, it was too late.

The warning signs had come the year before. Now they had learned to keep their secret to themselves.

I remember Eric telling me once in class that he couldn't wait until he turned eighteen so he could buy a gun. The conversation was pretty short, and he didn't bring it up again. But when someone says something like that, you have no reason to think he might already own guns.

But Eric and Dylan did.

They bought their first guns with the help of Robyn, who appeared in that class picture next to us. We had first met Robyn as sophomores, when she was dating a guy in the theatre department. Since that time, she had remained friends with Dylan.

I never liked Robyn. I didn't talk to her much. I knew she had a romantic interest in Dylan, but he didn't return it. When they attended Prom together, it was only as friends. However, he and Eric did find a way to use her friendship to their advantage.

Eric and Dylan had tried to buy weapons at the Tanner Gun Show in Denver once before, but failed because they weren't eighteen. Their solution was to find someone who *was* eighteen to do their buying for them. So they found Robyn.

In police interviews, Robyn claimed Eric and Dylan had told her that the weapons were just for target practice, and that when she asked them whether they would be used for anything else, they replied that they weren't stupid enough to do such a thing. So, without further question, she accompanied them to the show, let them pick out the weapons, and then acted as the buyer. No one at the gun show seemed to question this.

In his journal, Eric described the events of the day this way:

> *Well, folks, today was a very important day in the history of R. Today, along with VoDkA and someone else who I won't name, we went downtown and purchased the following: a dou-*

ble barrel 12 ga. shotgun, a pump-action 12 ga. shotgun, a 9mm carbine, 250 9mm rounds, 15 12 ga. slugs, and 40 shotgun shells, 2 switchblade knives, and a total of 4-10 round clips for the carbine. We ... have ... GUNS! We fucking got em, you sons of bitches! HA! HA HA HA! Neener! Booga Booga. Heh. It's all over now. This caps it off, the point of no return ...

Later, we learned of many other warning signs that happened in that final year. However, they were so spread out in space and time that no one could think of putting them together.

The incidents later shared by people who knew Eric Harris and Dylan Klebold spell a tragic story, and if one person had known about all of them, an obvious—yet unthinkable—picture would have been painted.

Columbine student Nate Dykeman told police he had witnessed Eric and Dylan detonating a pipe bomb in January of 1998, the same day that the Denver Broncos won the Super Bowl. However, Nate also said Eric's father had found one of Eric's pipe bombs and confronted him with it. According to Nate, Eric showed him the bomb in his parents' closet and said that his dad was going to make him detonate it—but that his dad had never bothered to look for more of the bombs in Eric's room.

Nate Dykeman would drift apart from Eric after the two became interested in the same girl. However, Nate told police that in the weeks before the shootings Eric had showed him a videotape of himself and Dylan firing weapons alongside Mark Manes and Philip Duran. The tapes depicted both a TEC-9 and a sawed-off shotgun. Neither of those weapons would be ideal for target shooting, yet that's what Eric told Nate they were doing.

Chris Morris, a member of the "Trench Coat Mafia" who still worked with Eric and Dylan at Blackjack Pizza, told police that Eric had joked about killing jocks and suggested placing bombs on the generators as a way to blow up the school. However, it had seemed like joking around, Morris said.

Classmates in Eric's government class recall a video he and Dylan shot for "The Trench Coat Mafia Protection Service," in which the two offered their services to the bullied and oppressed; they could be hired to beat up a bully or wreak havoc on an enemy.

Eric's parents, who were told by doctors that he was struggling with depression, had placed him on Luvox.

Dylan wrote a paper for his sixth-period composition class called "The Mind and Motives of Charles Manson" in November of 1998. Months later, he would turn in an essay to his creative writing teacher that graphically described a trenchcoat-wearing assassin shooting and killing bullies outside a bar.

A co-worker remembers Eric receiving a paycheck in March and commenting that he would use it to buy more propane tanks. The co-worker told police that Eric already owned seven tanks and wanted to get nine more with the check, aiming to have thirty in all by April 20. The employee asked why; Eric replied that it was Hitler's birthday.

Nicole Markham, who dated Chris Morris and went to Columbine, told police that she saw Eric and Dylan standing in the school cafeteria with a piece of paper they were studying intently. When she asked what it was, they refused to tell her, so she playfully grabbed it away from them. She saw that it was a homemade diagram of the cafeteria, with the location of the security cameras clearly marked.

Each of these warning signs, by themselves, seemed little more than odd to the people who observed them. Put together, they form a disturbing picture of what was about to happen.

No one was in a position to put them together.

When I look back, I'm still amazed at the acting job Eric and Dylan did. None of us knew what was going to happen. None of us knew that for over a year they'd been cooking up a plot to attack the school.

Some of my classmates talked to the media about how Eric and Dylan used to sit in class and say things like "Can I shoot that guy?" I remember them saying things like that, too. However, it never seemed serious. After all, there are jokes about violence, and then there are actual threats to commit violence. Eric and Dylan always seemed like they were joking. They would see some jock push a kid over, or hear a kid say something completely ignorant and stupid, and say, "Boy, that fucker should be killed," or "I wish that guy would get hit by a car." They were general expressions of frustration. They never said anything like "Boy, I'm going to go home and get my .22 and put a bullet in his brain this afternoon." It never seemed serious.

Some have suggested that Eric and Dylan never seriously thought they were going to do it until right before they actually did. I don't agree. They knew exactly what they were doing. There's a part of me that would like to believe that Dylan was separating himself emotionally from what was about to happen. Realistically, though, that's not likely. He and Eric both wanted revenge. They had been looking forward to April 20 for a long, long time.

A few months before graduation, parents of seniors at Columbine High School were required to attend a meeting explaining how the ceremony would be carried out. Attendance was required in order to get tickets to the ceremony. So Judy Brown called Sue Klebold, and the two made plans to attend together.

After they had listened to the speech and picked up their tickets, the two longtime friends sat down in the auditorium to catch up. It was their first real conversation in months. Judy learned that Dylan's father had taken him to visit the University of Arizona, where he was enrolled for the fall. Dylan had seen his future dorm room and the student lounge, and taken a walking tour of the campus.

"She was so excited about how Dylan was doing," Judy recalled of Mrs. Klebold. "Dylan was picking out his room, and he was looking at the girls and talking about them; it was something he had never really done before. He would nudge his dad and say, 'Ooo, she was gorgeous; did you see her?'

"She said he was so happy that Dylan was on his way," Judy continued. "She asked him, 'Are you sure you want to take off like this, to a big college? Do you maybe just want to break away slowly instead?' But he wanted to go. He picked out a dorm room that was going to be near the cafeteria. He talked about how great the campus was. He was excited.

"He loved computers, and now he was going to computer school. He was planning on going to the Prom. It was so unlike him, seeing him coming out of his shell like this. It seemed like he was happy, like he was finding his way."

Judy paused for a moment before continuing.

"And all the while, he was planning this massacre."

The key point I have to stress about those final few weeks at Columbine is that, to me, nothing seemed out of the ordinary. All of the warning signs I saw had happened back in junior year. While friends did observe the occasional odd thing, it was like holding one tiny puzzle piece and trying to figure out what the picture might be. It would all make sense later, but at the time, Eric and Dylan were covering their tracks well.

Dylan wasn't the only one who seemed to be making plans for his future. Eric had applied to join the Marines; the son of an Air Force veteran, he talked often that semester about his desire to serve in the military, and how the idea of being paid to run around with guns and defend America really appealed to him.

On April 15, 1999, Eric and his parents met with a Marine recruiter to discuss Eric's application. Eric was told that his application was being rejected because he had lied and told them he wasn't taking Luvox to treat depression. Because of that—and perhaps because Eric hadn't disclosed his medical history regarding his chest deformity—the military was turning him down.

Eric mentioned that at school the next day. It was the Friday before the attack on Columbine. He seemed disappointed, even though he talked like he was blowing it off.

Sometimes I wonder if, had he been accepted, Eric would have been prompted to make a last-minute change in plans and abort the attack. We will never know the answer to that. On the other hand, it's possible that the entire application was a ruse, just like Dylan's application to college; after all, if two boys look like they are actively planning for their futures, would you ever suspect that they were actually plotting a massacre that would end in their own deaths?

Some adults ask how high schoolers could have been mature enough to carry out such a detailed plan in secret. These people are selling teenagers short. Teenagers—particularly intelligent ones like Eric and Dylan—are more than capable of keeping their intentions secret, especially if they have been planning something for a long time. A lot of strategy can be discussed in a year, and if one of the plotters starts to get sloppy, the other can pull him back into line.

Their plan was amazing in its intricacy. Eric and Dylan had spent over a year working at Blackjack Pizza to save up the money to buy weapons, which they managed through close friends. Had Eric and Dylan been acting like homicidal maniacs when they asked for help with the guns, their friends would have been suspicious. However, because they were acting so much more mature, it seemed believable that they only wanted the weapons for target practice. From there, they went "target shooting" for the next few months—to teach themselves how to shoot.

They kept their weapons hidden; nothing was ever left out where their parents would see it, because Eric had already learned his lesson with the pipe bomb.

Rather than act like rebels, they put on their best behavior. Eric, who used to shoot his mouth off on his Web site about the violence he wanted to create, had learned to shut up. He kept his plans to his personal journal now, which no one would see but him—at least, not until the plan had been executed.

In his journals, Eric wrote, "If I have to cheat and lie to everyone, then that's fine. THIS is what I am motivated for, THIS is my goal, THIS is what I want 'to do with my life.' "

On April 3 of 1999, Eric wrote this final entry in his journal:

> Months have passed. It's the first Friday night in the final month. Much shit has happened. VoDkA has a TEC-9, we test fired all of our babies, we have 6 time clocks ready, 39 crickets, 24 pipe bombs, and the napalm is under construction ... The amount of dramatic irony and foreshadowing is fucking amazing. Everything I see and hear, I incorporate into NBK somehow. Either bombs, clocks, guns, napalm, killing people, anything and everything finds some tie to it. Feels like a goddamn movie sometimes. I wanna try to put some bombs and mines around this town too, maybe. Get a few extra frags on the scoreboard. I hate you people for leaving me out of so many fun things. And

no, don't fucking say "Well that's your fault" because it isn't, you people had my phone #, and I asked and all, but no no no no don't let the weird looking Eric KID come along, ooh fucking nooo ...

That final week, life proceeded as normal. People were talking Prom at school, but I didn't care too much. I knew Dylan was going with Robyn and that people were trying to hook Eric up with a date. He asked a few girls, but they all turned him down. In the end, he wound up inviting a girl over to his house on Prom night to watch a movie, then catching up with Dylan later at the after-Prom party.

Me, I had to work that night; I had a job as a manager at Pizza Hut. Besides, I had just broken up with my longtime girlfriend only a few weeks beforehand. Prom was the last thing on my mind.

Two days later, Becca and I asked Eric and Dylan if they wanted to skip fourth hour and meet us for lunch at McDonald's. Eric said sure, but that he and Dylan were going to stop by Eric's house first. We skipped class a lot; it was only a little more than a month until graduation, after all. We were high school seniors at the end of the year, looking past Columbine at what lay ahead. We were ready to get out of that school. Ready to get on with our lives.

It was April 19, 1999.

According to the initial Jefferson County Sheriff's Report, released to the media one year after the Columbine tragedy occurred, Dylan Klebold wrote an entry in his notebook late on the night of Sunday, April 18.

"About 26.5 hours from now, the judgment will begin," Dylan reportedly wrote. "Difficult but not impossible, necessary, nerve-wracking and fun. What fun is life without a little death? It's interesting, when I'm in my human form, knowing I'm going to die. Everything has a touch of triviality to it."

Dylan also wrote out his itinerary for April 20, including when he would be meeting Eric, how they would fill their propane tanks, and when and where they would gear up.

Zach Heckler told police that on Monday, April 19, he called Dylan at around 10:30 p.m., as he often did. On his first try, the report says, Dylan was on the phone with someone else. On the second attempt, Dylan told Zach he was tired and not in the mood to talk. Heckler told police it seemed odd, because Dylan didn't usually go to bed until 12:30 or 1:00.

Police also report that on the same night, Eric recorded a message into a tape recorder.

"It will happen in less than nine hours now," he said. "People will die because of me ... It will be a day that will be remembered forever."

Tuesday morning. April 20. For once I didn't oversleep.

Aaron and I got into his car and headed for school. Now that he had his license too, we were alternating who drove. My class was playing dodgeball in P.E. today, so once we pulled into a spot at Clement Park, I headed for the gymnasium.

Nothing seemed unusual until I arrived in third hour. I sat down next to Becca Heins, who asked me if I knew where Eric was.

I shrugged. Maybe he and Dylan went downtown or something, I said. Both of us were astonished that Eric was skipping today's test on Chinese philosophy.

The same was true when I arrived in fourth hour. No Eric, no Dylan. Strange that neither of them had mentioned their plans to skip. We had no idea where they were.

Somewhere between 10:30 and 11:00 a.m., Eric and Dylan were at Eric's house, making final preparations. Their weapons complete and assembled, their bombs packed into duffel bags, all that was left was for them to record one last message on videotape.

While the actual tape has never been released to the public, members of the media were allowed to view it, and much of their conversation was also described in police reports.

"It's about half an hour before our little judgment day," Dylan said into the camera. "Just know that I'm going to a better place than here. I didn't like life too much, and I know I'll be happier wherever the fuck I go. So I'm gone."

Dylan also held the camera for Eric, who had his own parting words.

"I just wanted to apologize to you guys for any crap," Eric said. "To everyone I love, I'm really sorry about all of this. I know my mom and dad will be just fucking shocked beyond belief."

From behind the camera, Dylan spoke up. "We did what we had to do."

The two made their final comments to friends, then Eric ended the tape. "That's it," he said. "Goodbye."

Fourth hour ended, and I walked outside to have a cigarette. I went down to the sidewalk at the edge of Pierce Street, looked to the south—and saw a little Honda pull into the Columbine parking lot.

Eric.

I never saw Dylan pull in. I had no idea of what was going to happen. I was still a high school kid whose biggest concern at the moment was whether or not to skip fifth hour.

So many things about that day are a blur. But I remember one thing clearly.

I remember Eric Harris—the kid who had threatened to kill me, the kid who was now carrying lethal weaponry in duffel bags on the ground next to me—laughing as he told me to go home.

Part Two

AFTERMATH

12

the nightmare begins

WHEN BROOKS OBSERVED ERIC HARRIS PULLING DUFFEL BAGS OUT OF his car, he couldn't have known that those duffel bags contained explosives, including two massive propane bombs. The bombs were hidden by gym clothes, so that anyone who got suspicious and looked inside the bag wouldn't see anything amiss. After Eric spoke with Brooks, the killers placed those two bombs in the cafeteria. Their timers were set to go off at the exact time that they calculated the highest number of students would be eating lunch.

The two had parked their cars outside two of the lower-level entrances to Columbine. They had additional bombs rigged in the cars, timed to go off exactly half an hour later—right around the time that police and rescue personnel would be on the scene.

If things went according to plan, the cafeteria bombs would go off, killing hundreds and doing massive damage to the school itself. Eric and Dylan wanted to be waiting outside, wearing black trench coats with their weapons concealed underneath, to pick off survivors as they emerged from the carnage.

However, the timed bombs failed.

Waiting outside, Eric and Dylan realized something was wrong. Witnesses saw them standing atop the west staircase overlooking the school, perhaps deciding what to do next. Underneath their trench coats, *they were armed with pipe bombs, cricket bombs, the two shotguns, Eric's Hi-Point 9-millimeter carbine, and Dylan's TEC-9.*

One of them shouted to the other, "Go! Go!"

Brooks's brother Aaron was eating lunch in the cafeteria at the time. He remembers everything seeming normal until a few kids stood up and began gathering around the windows, pointing at something. When Aaron looked, he saw two kids already lying on the ground, and he watched another collapse and lie still.

"No one knew what was happening," he said. "We didn't see any blood. We thought maybe it was a fight."

Then teacher Dave Sanders ran through the cafeteria, shouting at students to get down and take cover under the tables. Aaron turned to a friend and laughed. "You have any idea what's going on?"

That's when he heard the crack of gunshots. Aaron and his friends dropped to their knees and started crawling along the floor. When they heard another series of gunshots, they got up and ran. They tore through the auditorium, coming out in the hallway on the other side and getting swept up in the massive crush of students fleeing for the exit.

Aaron didn't look back at the shooters. He could hear them; bullets were flying over his head. From somewhere behind him, Aaron heard another student scream, "I'm shot!" Ahead of him, bullets shattered the glass in the entrance doors.

Aaron made it out safely and ran to his car with his friends. They drove home as fast as they could.

Others were not so lucky. Two students, Rachel Scott and Daniel Rohrbough, lay dead outside the west entrance of Columbine. Sean Graves, Lance Kirklin, Michael Johnson, Mark Taylor, and Anne Marie Hochalter had all been injured, several of them critically.

According to the Jefferson County Sheriff's report, witnesses heard one of the gunmen shout, "This is what we always wanted to do. This is awesome!"

Thank God. Thank God.

Those were the only words going through my head as I ran from the car to my house. My little brother was alive. I threw my arms around him and cried.

I looked around. Aaron had a few friends standing around. I hugged them, too. I was happy to see anyone I knew. If I saw them, that meant that they were alive, that there was one less death at my school.

I went inside and sat down in front of the TV, which was already on. There was Columbine, all over every channel. Aerial shots, ground shots, and every kind of media you could imagine.

And then there was a picture I'll never forget. Sarah Bay appeared on the screen. She was alive. I realized that this TV was my window into who was making it out safely.

So I kept watching.

Teacher Patti Nielsen, who was serving as hall monitor that day, was approached by student Brian Anderson about some sort of activity going on outside. She told police she walked to the glass doors of the west entrance and saw Eric Harris with a gun—and that at first she believed it to be a toy, perhaps part of a prank of some kind.

Harris turned and looked at her, then opened fire. The bullets shattered the glass and grazed Nielsen's shoulder. Fragments also hit Anderson. The two turned and ran for the Columbine library, where Nielsen dialed 911.

Several police officers—including Deputy Neil Gardner, the officer assigned to the school—arrived on scene and exchanged gunfire with Eric Harris. However, they did not pursue the gunmen into the school.

Friends kept coming over to my house as the afternoon progressed. My cousin Josh Ellis left work and came by to see me; he had heard the news on the radio. My friend Mike Troutman, who was a student at Heritage High School nearby, got out of school early and came over. Trevor Dolac came by. As each of my friends arrived, I thanked them for coming and we hugged, but I was so numb that, to be honest, I remember little of what we said. Nothing felt real about that day.

We knew that Eric was involved in the shooting, but we weren't sure about Dylan. That really had my mom frightened. We were hearing reports on the news of multiple shooters, "clad in black," and we all knew that wherever Eric went, Dylan was sure to be somewhere nearby.

Now that she knew Aaron and I were both safe, my mom thought of her friend Sue Klebold. She had spoken with the Klebolds briefly on the phone; they had already heard the rumors. Since Aaron and I had our dad there, my mom decided to drive to the Klebold house to offer her friend support.

We were hoping it would turn out that Dylan wasn't involved. But logic told us otherwise. Dylan had skipped class with Eric. No one had seen or heard from him since the shooting started. It looked bad.

My fears were confirmed as I saw Dylan's name appear on the screen. He was one of two suspects; the other was Eric. I felt my heart sink into the floor.

Right at that moment, the phone rang. It was my mother. She was with the Klebolds, standing outside the house. A police detective was already at the Klebold home.

"Have you heard anything?" she asked me. "Do they know who the shooters are?"

I took a moment. "Mom, it's Dylan."

"Are you sure? I mean, do you know that for sure or is that just what someone said?"

"Mom, they just showed his name on the TV. It's Dylan."

While their parents and friends were in anguish over what was happening, Eric and Dylan were in the library, alone amidst the carnage they had made.

Ten more people were now dead. Dave Sanders—the teacher who had warned Aaron Brown and hundreds of other students in the cafeteria to run—was still alive, but had been badly wounded in the hallway. He had made it to one of the science rooms, where he now lay bleeding to death as students tried frantically to save him. He would be dead in another few hours, becoming Eric and Dylan's thirteenth victim.

Ten students had been killed in the Columbine library. Shortly after Patti Nielsen made her 911 call, Eric and Dylan came through the library doors with guns in hand. They took their time picking off victims one by one, shooting under desks, executing kids, and laughing.

The police knew this because Nielsen's 911 call was still open. She had set the phone down and taken cover under the library counter, so the receiver was still picking up everything. Even though fire alarms were ringing throughout the school, thanks to the multiple pipe bombs Eric and Dylan had lobbed into the cafeteria, police could hear the screams, the gunshots, and the taunts.

The police weren't moving. Later they explained that they had been trained to establish a perimeter around a suspect, ensuring that there could be no escape. However, no one was actually entering the school to try to engage the shooters, even though the 911 call offered a clear indication of where they were in the building.

Because police weren't pressuring them, Eric and Dylan left the library—allowing thirty-four students to escape out the back door in the process—and went downstairs to the cafeteria. Security cameras recorded Eric attempting to set off one of the failed propane bombs by shooting at it with his shotgun. He had no luck. The tape also captured Dylan lobbing one last pipe bomb, creating a fire in the cafeteria. Then the pair returned to the library for the final time.

One of the first things Aaron did once he got home was go to the computer and make sure we had a saved copy of Eric's Web site. Somehow, even amidst the shock of what was happening, we knew we had something that people needed to know about.

I remember hearing one of the television reporters say that, according to police and school officials, "the suspects had no history of violence." That upset me. So we called the news hotline for one of the TV stations, wanting to correct them. When I told them about the Web pages and my history with Eric Harris, they asked if they could send a crew out to speak with me.

Half an hour later, reporter Ward Lucas from Channel 9 was knocking on our door.

We sat on the porch, and I told him what I knew. I showed him copies of Eric's Web site. I told him about my last meeting with Eric in the parking lot. I talked about the Trench Coat Mafia, and about how the group had been bullied by the jocks. Basically, I was rambling, trying to get points across even though I was still freaked out by everything.

Lucas was very kind. He said what he could to make me feel at ease. He thanked me for having come forward. Looking back, I think he felt sorry for me.

Once that interview hit the airwaves, other reporters started calling. The *Denver Post* wanted to talk. So did the *Rocky Mountain News.* Clips from Ward Lucas's interview with me were on CNN. For the first time, people were hearing what the police had known for a long time: Eric Harris was a dangerous kid.

Through it all, we still didn't know the details of what was happening at Columbine. We still watched events unfold on TV. I saw the live shot of Patrick Ireland crawling out the library window and being rescued. He had been shot multiple times, in the head and elsewhere.

The police were still waiting outside the school. We knew nothing about Eric and Dylan's fate. But deep down, I knew how this was going to end.

Perhaps Eric and Dylan had dreamed of dying in a glorious final shootout with police, and were disappointed that none were coming in. No one will ever know.

Four hours after the shooting began, Eric and Dylan would be found dead in a corner of the library—killed by self-inflicted gunshot wounds to the head.

The carnage they left was staggering. By now, Dave Sanders had succumbed to his injuries, despite the efforts of students who dialed 911, put up a sign in the window saying "1 Bleeding To Death," and waited for hours for help to come.

The ten library victims included Cassie Bernall, Steven Curnow, Corey DePooter, Kelly Fleming, Matthew Kechter, Daniel Mauser, Isaiah Shoels, John Tomlin, Lauren Townsend, and Kyle Velasquez. Nearly two dozen more students were injured.

I knew Eric and Dylan were dead long before they announced it on TV. Still, actually hearing the newscasters say it made it real.

My friends were gone. They had murdered other friends before they went. They had set off bombs and shot at the cops.

Yesterday we had skipped class to eat lunch together at McDonald's.

I couldn't even get my mind around something like that.

Parents were gathering at Leawood Elementary School, waiting for lists to be put up of kids who had been accounted for by the authorities. They waited for school buses that might or might not have been carrying their children out of danger.

Some parents waited through the night, finally realizing after the last bus had left that their children hadn't made it.

It wouldn't be until the next day that we would hear confirmed lists of the dead. The bodies wouldn't even be removed from the school that night. Students and parents alike could do little more than guess about who had lived and who hadn't.

Our family survived the attack. But another nightmare was just beginning.

The exterior of Columbine High School near the west entrance. Eric Harris and Dylan Klebold would begin their shooting rampage of April 20, 1999 in the area near the top of the stairs at left before entering the school.

Dylan Klebold (left) and Brooks Brown, age
eight, attend a meeting of the Cub Scouts.

Brooks (right) and Dylan enjoy a moment of playing together in the park during their elementary school days.

As young boys in Littleton, one of the interests Brooks and Dylan shared was a love of music. In this photo, the two sixth-grade boys perform in a band at a local talent show. Brooks, left, was on saxophone, while Dylan played the drums.

Dylan, age seventeen, shares a memory of the high school theatre program as Brooks Brown records him behind Blackjack Pizza, where Klebold and Eric Harris held part-time jobs, in late 1998.

Dylan and Brooks use the *Frankenstein* program to "roast" their fellow cast and crew members on a tribute video they recorded in late 1998.

Dylan and Brooks blow a kiss to the camera.

Brooks, foreground, poses for the 1999 Columbine senior class photo, with Eric and Dylan behind him. By the time this photo was taken, in the spring of 1999, Eric and Dylan were in the final stages of their plan to attack the school.

For their second class photo, the seniors at Columbine were given the chance to "get crazy" for the cameras. Here, Brooks, Eric, and Dylan pretend to aim guns at the camera. While the gesture was made in good fun at the time, one of the investigators in the Jefferson County Sheriff's Office would later point to the photo as a reason to suspect Brooks as an accomplice in the Columbine killings.

The Columbine High School yearbook photos of Eric Harris (left) and Dylan Klebold (right)

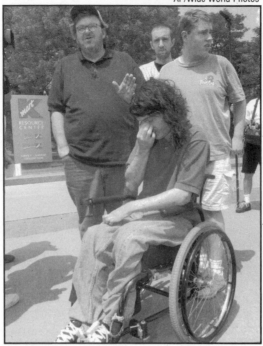

From left, author and filmmaker Michael Moore address-
es the media alongside Brooks Brown and Columbine
shooting victims Richard Castaldo (in wheelchair) and
Mark Taylor outside the Kmart corporate headquarters in
Michigan in 2001. Moore recruited the Columbine students to assist in a successful effort to convince Kmart
to remove handgun ammunition from its shelves.

Brooks shares a lighthearted moment with his parents, Randy and
Judy, at the Browns' home in Littleton, Colorado.

Page from Randy Brown's police report, March, 1998.

JEFFERSON COUNTY SHERIFF'S DEPARTMENT - OFFENSE / INCIDENT REPORT

CASE REPORT # 98-5504

□ OFFENSE ☑ INCIDENT □ CONTINUATION □ SUPPLEMENT / ORIGINAL VICTIM:

OFFENSE / INCIDENT CLASSIFICATION: SUSPICIOUS INCIDENT   STATUTE #   CURRENT CODE 80-181   □ FELONY □ MISDEMEANOR □ PETTY OFFENSE

		MONTH	DAY	YEAR	TIME	LOCATION OF OCCURRENCE BUSINESS NAME:
DATE / TIME	REPORTED	03	18	98	1720	ADDRESS
DATE / TIME OCCURRED	ON OR BETWEEN:	03	18	98	1720	CITY / CROSS 1 / CROSS 2

CODES: V - VICTIM   RP - REPORTING PARTY   W - WITNESS   SB - SUBJECT   PG - PARENT / GUARDIAN   RO - REGISTERED OWNER

CODE: RP — BROWN RANDY BROOKS — SAME AS 600

CODE: W — BROWN BROOKS — AGE 17 — SAME AS 600 — COLUMBINE H.S.

CODES: S - SUSPECT   SB - SUBJECT   MP - MISSING PERSON   RU - RUNAWAY   NCIC: CCIC:

CODE: SB1 — HARRIS ERIC AKA "REB" — LITTLETON CO 80123 — COLUMBINE H.S.

CODE: SB2 — KLEBOLD DYLAN AKA "VODKA" — LITTLETON CO 80127 — COLUMBINE H.S.

VEHICLE

□ SUSPECT □ VICTIM □ STOLEN □ OTHER

INDICATORS: □ GANG □ GAMING □ ALCOHOL □ DENVER MTN. □ DOMESTIC VIO. □ SHOPLIFT □ HATE CRIME / ANTI- □ S □ JUVENILE CASE

ASSIGNED TO: JC-001-010356

COPIES TO: DEP. GARDNER   COLUMBINE S.R.O.

PAGE: 1 OF 2

M. MELLER   BADGE # 3726

Page from Randy Brown's police report, March, 1998.

CONTINUATION ☒   SUPPLEMENT ☐   Connecting Case Report No.   Reporting Agency   Reporting Officer   Case Report   98-5504   AUTOMATED   Date This Report   03 18 98
Classification ☐ Suspicious Incident   Offense Status: Open ☐   Exceptionally Cleared ☐   Recommend Case: Review ☐   Cleared by Arrest ☐   Unfounded ☐   Closure ☐
Item No. | Quantity | Brand Name | Description | Serial No. | Value Stolen | Value Recovered | Value Damaged

NARRATIVE:

AT ABOUT 1710 I CONTACTED (RP) BROWN AT HES RESIDENCE. HE TOLD ME THAT (SBI) HARRIS, WHO GOES TO SCHOOL WITH HES SON (W) BROWN, WAS MAKING DEATH THREATS TOWARDS HES SON. (RP) BROWN TOLD ME THAT (SBI) HARRIS HAS HES OWN WEB PAGE (HTTP://MEMBERS.AOL.COM/REBDOOMIRE/INDEX.HTML) AND HAS MADE DEATH THREATS ON HES WEB PAGE TOWARDS HES SON (W) BROWN. (RP) BROWN ALSO TOLD ME THAT (SBI) HARRIS ALSO TALKS OFTEN OF MAKING PIPE BOMBS AND USING THEM TO KILL NUMEROUS PEOPLE. (RP) BROWN GAVE ME 10 PAGES OF MATERIAL HE HAS COPIED FROM (SBI) HARRIS' WEB PAGE. WHILE I OBSERVED THE COPIES I NOTICED THAT (SBI) HARRIS REFERRED TO "WANTING TO KILL" (W) BROWN THREE TIMES. (SBI) HARRIS ALSO EXPLAINED ABOUT MAKING AND DETONATING PIPE BOMBS AND USING THEM AGAINST PEOPLE. (RP) BROWN TOLD ME HE WAS CONCERNED FOR HES SON'S SAFETY. HE TOLD ME THAT HE HAS REPORTED (SBI) HARRIS TO J.C.S.D. OVER A YEAR AGO AND THAT IS WHY (SBI) HARRIS WANTS REVENGE AGAINST HES SON. HE TOLD ME HE WAS VERY INTERESTED IN REMAINING ANONYMOUS IN MAKING THIS REPORT. AND DID NOT WANT (SBI) HARRIS OR (SBI) KLEBOLD TO HAVE KNOWLEDGE ABOUT HES REPORTING THEM. (RP) BROWN TOLD ME THAT (SBI) KLEBOLD IS AN ACQUAINTANCE OF (SBI) HARRIS' AND DOES HAVE KNOWLEDGE ABOUT HES MAKING PIPE BOMBS. (RP) BROWN TOLD ME THAT IN THE PAST (SBI) HARRIS' HAS TALKED ABOUT CRIMES THAT HE HAS COMMITTED IN DETAIL ON HES WEB PAGE. (RP) BROWN SUBMITTED COPIES OF (SBI) HARRIS' WEB PAGE - ATTACHED

DISPOSITION:

A.O.D. FORWARD TO INVESTIGATIONS.

JC-001-010357

Officer Signature   Unit 247   Number 312   Supervisor Initials and Date   COPIES TO: DEP. GARDNER COLUMBINE S.R.O.   Page 2 of 2
81 ASAF 3 (Rev. 6/82)

Page from Randy Brown's police report, March, 1998.

98-5504

Pipe Bombs :

Eric Harris -
"REB"

Dylan Klebold -
"VODKA"   Rd.
                              80127

    Eric Harris + Dylan Klebold
have made and detonated
pipe bombs. Eric Harris is
the instigator.
    See internet info.

HTTP://members.aol.com/rebdomine/index.html
            rebdoomer

photo by Rob Merritt

Two years after she was killed, flowers and cards continue to adorn the gravesite of Columbine student Rachel Scott in Littleton, Colorado on April 20, 2001. Rachel was one of Eric and Dylan's first victims.

13

PEOPLE HAVE ASKED ME IF, IN THOSE INITIAL HOURS AFTER THE massacre, I stopped to wonder why Eric had let me leave the school. The truth is, the question didn't even enter my mind until later. That day, my mind was solely occupied with trying to find out who was still alive.

Trevor and I left my house and started driving around, looking for familiar faces anywhere we could find them. It didn't matter who they were; every person we saw was one more person who had survived. We went to Leawood Elementary, where lists of students who were confirmed as alive and safe were being posted. We went to the Perkins restaurant. We drove around the neighborhood looking for big groups of people.

No matter where we went, I'd find somebody I knew. It didn't matter who it was; we'd throw our arms around each other in relief and cry.

I remember seeing people like Andy Robinson, Chris Logan, and Dan Berg. I grabbed Zach Heckler in a massive hug.

"Thank God you're alive," we'd say.

There was one person we were looking for more than any other. We'd heard a rumor that Rachel Scott was among those who'd been killed. We'd been at home watching helicopter footage outside the school, and lying near the exterior steps of Columbine was the body of a girl who was wearing clothes just like those I'd seen Rachel wearing earlier that day.

147

My brother Aaron was on the phone all afternoon, asking people if they knew anything. I was sitting with my friend Steve Partridge on our porch when Aaron ran out to give us an update.

"Rachel Scott's dead," he said.

Aaron was just giving us a name. He didn't realize that we both knew Rachel, or that Steve had dated Rachel for a long time. When Steve heard the news, he fell silent. Then he collapsed.

We tried to hold out hope. We knew Aaron was getting his information from gossip; no names had been released yet by the police. There was still a chance.

That night, we scanned through every crowd. We asked around. "Have you seen Rachel? Do you know if she made it out?" No one had an answer.

Rachel was special to me for one reason: she defied every expectation I'd ever had of a Christian.

We had our first real conversation at State Qualifiers for speech and debate that year. We'd seen each other around before that, but hadn't spoken much. In looking back, that's kind of an odd thing; after all, we were both in speech, both actors in the Columbine theatre program, and she'd been dating my friend Steve for nearly a year. Later she would go to Prom with Nick Baumgart. Yet through all that, we never seemed to cross paths.

Part of the problem was that I knew Rachel was a devout Christian. I never made it a secret in high school that I wasn't a religious person, and devout Christians used to come after me and tell me I was going to hell. They would use quotes from the Bible to throw insults at me. I'd seen them try to force their beliefs on other students, guilting them into it, pressuring them to join up. They didn't want to hear what you thought about God, or the world. All they wanted to hear was "Jesus Christ is my Savior"—and if we didn't agree, we weren't worth associating with.

I didn't want to be criticized for my beliefs. So I never thought I had a reason to make conversation with Rachel Scott. At least, not until that afternoon at Speech Contest.

I'd stepped outside for a cigarette in between rounds; smokers generally tended to congregate in one single area at contests. When I walked out, Rachel was there, too, standing alone next to the building with a Marlboro Light.

"Hey," she said when she saw me. "How'd it go?"

We struck up a conversation; it wasn't long before the subject shifted over to faith. It's a topic I get into quite often with people. Yet as we spoke, I realized that Rachel was different from other kids at Columbine for one reason: she listened.

It was a first. I can't think of any time before that when a Christian asked me about my beliefs without interrupting constantly, or running right over my ideas, or just sitting there and snickering. Yet Rachel wasn't like that at all. Rachel listened to me speak about Taoism and my problems with the Bible and the church. She was genuinely interested, and didn't seem to judge me for it.

She talked about her own beliefs as well, but not in an attempt to convert me. She was just explaining, and I listened carefully, just as she had done for me. Then we started casually debating the subject.

"Where does your faith in God come from?" I asked. "After all, you don't see God, right? So how can you be sure that he really exists?"

"I can see him," she replied. "I know that God is real. I know it in my heart. You can only believe in what you know to be true. You know your own truth. I know mine. Everyone should be able to find that within themselves."

"But with most Christians I know, it's not like that," I said. "They think their way is the only way to live, and when you tell them you don't agree then they'll just tell you that you're going to hell. I mean, seriously—do you believe that it's your role as a Christian to try and save everyone else?"

Rachel shook her head. "It's not about that for me," she said. "I'm not trying to go out there and convert people. I just want to be an example. I want to live my life for God, and let other people take from that whatever they want."

I took a drag of my cigarette, mulling that over.

"You ever read the *Tao te Ching*?" I asked.

Rachel shook her head no.

"Well, basically it argues that the greatest teacher teaches without teaching," I continued. "I don't know. You kind of sound like you're not so much Christian as Taoist."

Rachel didn't say anything. She just smiled.

It amazed me. The fact that we could sit there, two people on such opposite sides of the spectrum of faith, and talk openly about our differences the way that we did—it wasn't something I'd seen before at Columbine. I couldn't get over how open and honest Rachel Scott was. In my mind, Rachel was an example of what the ideal Christian should be.

Rachel's beliefs were strong, yet she accepted people who felt differently. She felt that the path to spiritual enlightenment didn't mean scaring people, lecturing or judging them. She just lived her life the best way she knew how, and hoped other people would follow her example.

Imagine what a better place this world could have been throughout history if more people had shared Rachel Scott's viewpoint.

Rachel and I never talked about faith again after that; we each knew where the other stood, and stayed friends regardless. It was a refreshing change of pace as far as Christians were concerned; I discovered that I really enjoyed her company.

The last time I saw her was on April 20. She'd just appeared in the last play of the season, *Smoke in the Room*, in a role that had required her to cut her hair short and dye it. She was defying people's expectations to the end.

Rachel was eating lunch with another student, Richard Castaldo, when Eric and Dylan began their attack.

Rachel and Richard were the first two people hit. Rachel was struck twice in the legs and once in the torso; more bullets tore through Richard's spine, leaving him paralyzed.

What happened to Rachel next is a mystery. Richard's mother told NBC's Dateline that when Richard first came out of surgery, he described the scene in detail. He said Rachel was approached by the shooters a second time and asked if she believed in God. She said yes, and they killed her.

Later, Richard told police that he remembers Rachel lying on the ground, crying, and that the shooters approached a second time but left him for dead. However, he no longer remembered whether Rachel was asked about her faith in her final moments. To this day, he cannot recall what happened after he was shot.

"After he got the breathing tube out, he was crying and upset, telling me through sobs how they taunted and teased her about God," Castaldo's mother, Connie Michalik, told the Denver Rocky Mountain News on April 21, 2000. "Then he heard a shot and he didn't know what happened to her. He asked me again this morning: 'What did I say? Why didn't anybody write it down?' He's asked me so many times. Richard has cried a thousand tears for Rachel. He has so much guilt inside."

My parents went to Dylan's funeral. It was a small affair; only a hand-ful of people bothered to come out, and the ones who did were mainly there in support of the Klebold family. I heard that there were some nice tributes made there.

Rachel's funeral, the only one I attended in the wake of Columbine, couldn't have been any more different. It took place in a packed church only a few blocks south of Columbine, and was televised by CNN. The rat-ings during that funeral were higher than anything else CNN had previ-ously broadcast.

At first, I went to sit with the rest of the debate team. With dirty looks and whispered comments, they made it clear that they didn't want me there. These people, who had known me for years, had been with me to debate competitions, had been Rachel's and my teammates, were now turning their backs on me because I had been friends with Eric and Dylan.

"You're going to burn in hell," one of them told me.

I suppose that under different circumstances, I would have made some retort. Here we were, at a funeral for someone who had advocated kindness and acceptance; the kids who called themselves her friends weren't exactly following her example. But I didn't have the heart. I was too shocked. I just moved away from them and sat with Steve and Doug.

Just a few days ago, Steve and I had driven around looking for Rachel, hoping to find her alive. Now she was here, in a closed casket at the front of the church. It still didn't seem real.

There were several moments during that funeral that truly were beau-tiful. Rachel's sister did an exact recreation of the Christian dance Rachel had performed at the talent show the year before, accompanied by the song "Watch the Lamb and Who Nailed Him There."

When it came time for Rachel's friends to speak, Nick Baumgart gave a genuine, from-the-heart speech that focused on the positive memories we had of her.

"Her trueness to herself was amazing," Nick said. "She didn't let anybody affect who she was. She didn't let anybody tell her that what she believed and who she was wasn't okay. She was true to herself, and because of that, she was true to everybody else. In a sense, she is still here. She always will be, and that smile will still be here … I'm lucky to have known her. I'm fortunate to have been her friend, and I'm fortunate to have called her my Prom date. But I'm truly blessed to have had her in my life."

I was really moved by the beauty of the service … until Bruce Porter, the officiating minister, stepped up to give his speech.

Porter has since written a book called *The Martyr's Torch: The Message of the Columbine Massacre.* On the back cover of the book, Porter's bio describes him as "a 'man with a mission' to call Christians back to their ancient roots of fervent dedication and radical passion for Christ no matter what the cost."

That much was obvious at Rachel's funeral. With the CNN cameras rolling, Porter had come to turn the service into a recruiting rally.

"We've removed the Ten Commandments from our schools," he told us. "In exchange, we've reaped selfish indifference and glorified hedonism. We've told our children that they were nothing more than highly evolved amoebae, accidentally brought forth from a mud pool somewhere in time. And we wonder why so many of them see no intrinsic value to life.

"We removed prayer from our schools and we've reaped violence and hatred and murder," Porter continued. "And we have the fruit of those activities before us now. I want to say to you here today that prayer was established again in our public schools last Tuesday!" Applause rang out as Porter's volume increased. Porter went on to call Rachel a "martyr" who had now "dropped her torch and gone on to her eternal reward." He started asking who would pick it up for her, encouraging young people to "take your schools back."

"I want to know right now who will take up that torch," he said. "Let me see you. Who will pick up Rachel's torch? Who will do it? Hold it high!"

People in the church began to stand up. Kids and parents were cheering. At the podium, Porter was growing more feverish, more evangelical, as he started to address the TV cameras.

"Hold up that torch right now!" he went on, his voice rising. "If you are watching from some other place, stand up where you are. Stand up and say 'I won't be a victim! I will lift that torch high! The love of Jesus!' I want you to know that by doing that, you've declared a revolution!"

I sat there in stunned silence. This was wrong. To me, a funeral should be about loved ones remembering the person they've lost, and saying goodbye. Yet Porter had another goal in mind. In one of his own e-mails before the funeral—which he reprinted in his book—the minister wrote, "CNN will be broadcasting from the funeral as a part of a press pool, and there is every possibility that millions will be joining with us as we mourn Rachel and the other students who were slain. Pray that we will be able to speak into the hearts of multiplied millions of young people the reality of Christ's love for them ..."

Porter was using the incident of Rachel's death to convert as many young people to his faith as possible. This was a slap in the face to the scores of non-Christian kids who Rachel had befriended, including me.

Rachel was a Christian, yes. But she was all about acceptance, whether people looked different, acted different, or had different beliefs. She was about reaching out to the less fortunate in school and making them feel welcome. She was about living true to herself, and helping other people live true to themselves. She was about leading by example rather than by sermons. These were ideals that could be appreciated by many of her peers, regardless of their faith.

Porter noted in his speech that Rachel had reached out to people from all walks of life, and accepted them. If he knew this, then he had to expect that people from all walks of life would be at her funeral. Jewish. Agnostic. Atheist. People who were still discovering their beliefs. This funeral was for all of us to mourn together. It should not have been for harvesting new followers and making political statements.

If Porter had truly wanted to recognize Rachel's legacy, he could have pointed out how so many people had come to the service that day, or how so many kids wanted to speak in her memory. Perhaps he could have allowed more of them to do so.

Steve and I sat there for a moment, staring at the hundreds of people around us who were now standing and applauding. We didn't know what to say.

Then slowly, Steve stood up too, silent amidst the circus of cheering and clapping. He turned back and looked at me.

"Rachel's torch," he said quietly. "Not his."

When he said that, I stood up too. In honor of Rachel.

At the end of the funeral, as people were getting ready to file out, they asked the family to leave. No one was expecting what happened next.

They opened Rachel's casket.

There was Rachel. Dead. Her body, right there, in the casket for all to see. I don't know what they were trying to show people by doing this, but in order to exit, you had no choice but to walk right by it.

As we filed out, Doug was the first of our group to see her. He started crying. It was hard to watch.

Steve was next. He saw Rachel's body and collapsed on the floor in tears. Here was his former girlfriend, who still meant the world to him, and his body just failed him. Doug and I had to pick him back up and help him out of there. Of course, when I saw Steve lose it, I was right behind him. All the tears I hadn't cried up to that point came gushing out, just like everybody else, as I saw Rachel lying there in that coffin.

As we walked out, holding Steve, there was a literal wall of cameras and reporters waiting for us. Taking pictures of us, looking at us, video-taping us.

We just wanted it to be over.

14

no answers

THE DAYS AFTER THE MURDERS WERE A BLUR. I WANDERED AROUND in a daze most of the time, trying to comprehend the nightmare that had hit all of us.

There were no answers to be found.

Imagine your own best friend. Someone you've known for almost your whole life. Someone who used to laugh and tell you jokes, and showed you his new Wolf badge from Cub Scouts, and chased frogs with you around the creek behind your grade school on Friday afternoons. Someone who, just yesterday, you ditched school with. Someone you always thought you knew.

Now imagine that, from out of nowhere, that friend turns around and guns down over a dozen people. Classmates. Friends. People who are close to you.

It's something you could never have seen in your wildest nightmare, yet there it is. On the TV, the media are talking about your friends the same way they talk about Ted Bundy or Charles Manson. Investigative specials are tossing out details about your friend's childhood like some kind of Twilight-Zone-tinged episode of *This Is Your Life*. When your mind tries to take it in and make sense of it all, you realize that you can't. Hell, you can't even ask your friend for an explanation. Because he put a bullet in his brain right after he did it.

They'd gunned down Rachel. They'd gunned down Danny. Then they'd blown their own brains out right in the fucking library.

No one could have explained it. No one could have known.

Or could they? Could I? I *knew* Eric was dangerous. I knew from those Web pages. Those rants Eric had posted, the "Rebel Missions" he'd documented, the bombs, the threats. His desire to kill me a year ago, before we finally made peace. Had I not gone far enough? Had I missed a chance to intervene?

There was no way to collect my thoughts, either. No matter where I went, the scene was the same: reporters everywhere, police asking questions, classmates crying. Every TV channel showed Columbine exclusives, or Eric and Dylan's smiling faces, or analysts debating what the tragedy represented to society. Psychiatrists were showing up at gatherings, wanting us to come up and hug them, to tell them what we were thinking, what we were feeling, to pour our hearts out. We got stares from the people who didn't know what to say, tears from the people who did.

It seemed to me that I spent most of those first few days crying. The people who saw me then say that I was like some kind of zombie, physically there but with no life in my eyes. When I wasn't numb, I was curled up in a ball, sobbing. Not like me at all, believe me. But then, I really wasn't myself again for a long time.

The only place I really found solace was with a pen. The day after the killings, in the midst of the media barrage, I put my thoughts onto paper for the first time.

April 20, 1999

Today the school became one, but with fifteen less
Gaining only demons, meant to anger, to depress
We handled those demons, and rose over our hate

To see that finding love was all but too late
The ones that had fallen took from us their joy
Their sweet innocence of being a girl, being a boy
The ones who remained grew old in a day
For the mistakes of two boys, the rest had to pay
As we look back over the smiles and the tears
We know our memories will destroy the pain, over the years
Myself, I know, has been dealt an insane hand
But I know, eventually, I must take a stand
They may call us Columbine—in name we are
But the real name we earned surpasses Columbine by far
The only name I care about that the media was giving
Is the truth about who we are: WE THE LIVING.

There were still seventeen days left until graduation. We didn't know what was going to happen—whether the year would be written off completely, if we'd be attending another school, if anyone could focus on schoolwork in the wake of what had happened. We didn't even know if Columbine itself would remain standing. Some argued that if the school was destroyed, Eric and Dylan would have "won," while others said the memory would forever taint the building.

The night after the murders, administrators asked Columbine students to gather at West Bowles Community Church, not far from the school. The teachers were going to let us know what had been decided.

We learned that Columbine High School was far too damaged for us to return. It was probably a good thing, anyway. There was no way that some folks could set foot back inside that building. Instead, students would be finishing out the school year at Chatfield High School.

The teachers tried to tell us how we should be feeling about this. That we'd make it through. That "we are all Columbine." They were trying to help.

But we didn't need to be told what we were going through. We already knew. We were the ones who had lost classmates. We were the ones who were seeing photos of our friends' dead bodies on the front page of the newspaper. No one needed to talk us through how we were feeling. It was already there.

Eventually the teachers announced that they were leaving to discuss other matters. Students were sitting there, acting like they didn't care what happened to them next. Everyone was in shock.

Then something happened.

One kid got up and began speaking into the microphone. I don't remember anymore who it was, or what he said. But it caught people's attention. At last we were hearing from our own. It started a chain reaction. Another kid got up. Then another.

A couple of kids who saw me there said I should get up and speak. I'm not sure what made me do it, but something in me agreed.

I walked up to the microphone, and looked out into that sea of tears and red faces. These were people who had ignored me in the school hallways only days before. Now their eyes were trained on me. Waiting for what I would say.

I had nothing prepared. I just let myself go.

I'd been trained through debate to keep my emotions in check while I was speaking; up there at that microphone, it was all I could do to choke back tears. I tried to make it clear to everyone that what had happened on April 20 had happened to us, not to outsiders or school officials. I said that we shouldn't let anyone tell us how to feel about this, or how to react.

I told everyone that we were in this together. "But," I added, "It's US—the students—who decide what we're going through. We need to think about this for ourselves. Don't let the teachers dictate our thoughts to us anymore." It was our decision, I said. Each one of us could determine our own fate.

I heard students applauding as I walked off. I hoped I'd said something meaningful. Then I collapsed and cried on the floor of the church.

In the days that followed, I spent a lot of my time sitting in front of the TV, watching new reports come in. The things that I saw were news to me as much as they were to the rest of the world. They reported that Eric and Dylan had been planning this massacre for over a year, with Eric keeping a journal that detailed what was in store. It was reported that, had Eric and Dylan survived, they wanted to "hijack a plane and crash it into New York City."

I was hearing all of it for the first time.

The public, of course, wanted an enemy. They wanted someone to punish. You'd think that by killing themselves Eric and Dylan had denied them that enemy. But they found two anyway, in Mark Manes and Philip Duran.

Philip had worked with Eric and Dylan over at Blackjack Pizza. He told them, when they were looking for someone over eighteen who would buy guns for them, that he knew where they could get their hands on a TEC-9. He put them in touch with Mark, who sold the gun to Dylan for $500.

When that came out, the public was in an uproar. Philip and Mark were instantly branded as killers, and everyone wanted their heads. They were both arrested and convicted; each was sentenced to six years in prison.

There was also Robyn Anderson.

Immediately after the shootings, a lot of people reached out to Robyn. After all, she had been Dylan's Prom date. While Dylan hadn't had a girlfriend, a lot of people figured that Robyn was the closest thing to it. Kind of ironic; so many people wouldn't talk to me or Chris Morris or Zach Heckler, because we'd been friends with Eric and Dylan. But Robyn they embraced wholeheartedly.

Then the truth came out about what Robyn had done. Around the same time that the police found out about the TEC-9, they also discovered how Eric and Dylan had acquired their other weapons. Robyn admitted that she had given Eric and Dylan the weapons they needed to slaughter the class of 1999.

Did she face charges like Mark and Philip did? No. Not one. To this day, Robyn has never been charged with anything. Mark provided Eric and Dylan with one weapon, and he's in jail until 2005. Robyn got them three guns, and she's at home.

Funny how our system works.

The media were on top of these developments, along with everything else that was coming to light in the days after Columbine. Plenty of people in Littleton criticized the media for being too invasive and violating their privacy. But to be honest, I understood their predicament. They were good people who didn't want to be there any more than we did, but they had a job to do. There were some isolated examples of assholes, sure, but most of the people I met in the media were pretty cool to me. And it was their work that kept information coming out. If it had been up to the police and the school, any reports of bullying would have been suppressed, and the police would have kept quiet about our family's report on the Web pages. The questions about police response would have been pushed aside. It was the media who fought to keep that from happening.

I found myself talking to quite a few reporters in those first few days. After my first interview with Ward Lucas, they just started coming out of the woodwork. They mainly wanted to hear my story about the Web pages. They wanted to know more about these "warnings" the killers had left behind.

They also wanted to know about my last conversation with Eric. "What did he say? Did you see any guns with him? Why did he let you go? Why did he tell you to leave the school? Did you know what was going to happen?" They wanted to know if the rumors about bullying and cruelty at Columbine were true, and if they'd played any part in Eric and Dylan going over the edge.

I told them the truth; I didn't censor myself. Other kids were sugar-coating Columbine, making it sound like this peaceful, tranquil land of flowers and honey that Eric and Dylan had just walked into and shattered. "Oh, sure, there were jocks and everything," they'd say. "But it was never that bad. We just can't understand how this happened in a school like ours."

If people wanted to know what Columbine was like, I'd tell them. I'd tell them about the bullies who shoved the kids they didn't like into lockers, or called them "faggot" every time they walked past. I'd tell them about the jocks who picked relentlessly on anyone they considered to be below them. The teachers who turned a blind eye to the brutalization of their pupils, because those pupils weren't the favorites.

I told them about the way those who were "different" were crushed, and fights happened so regularly outside school that no one even paid attention. I told what it was like to live in constant fear of other kids who'd gone out of control, knowing full well that the teachers would turn a blind eye. After all, those kids were their favorites. We were the troublemakers.

"Eric and Dylan are the ones responsible for creating this tragedy," I told them. "However, Columbine is responsible for creating Eric and Dylan."

As I would later learn, this wasn't what I was supposed to say. I was supposed to jump on the bandwagon like everyone else. I was supposed to put aside what we'd all experienced over the past few years and pretend that Columbine was a wonderful place. Do you want to know the truth behind the slogan "We Are Columbine"? It's simple: We were still the same Columbine, where rumors determine truth and you don't go against the group mentality.

It was almost sad, the way some of my classmates defended the school. It was like an abused kid whose father dies after years of torturing him. That kid's not going to tell you the truth about his dad. He's going to defend his father and talk about how great he was. That's basically where things were with Columbine. Few people would speak the truth about the way it was. It was infuriating.

To be fair, I admit that there was one time I lied to the media to protect someone. Then again, when you consider who it was that I lied to, you can't exactly blame me. It was the day that *Inside Edition* came knocking on my door.

I said before that the media was pretty cool to me, and they were only there because they had to be. However, *Inside Edition* did not fit that description. Other reporters were moving carefully, trying to be sensitive when they talked to us. *Inside Edition* was there for one thing only, and that was the big scoop. We were all seeing pain and suffering. They were seeing dollar signs.

A few years ago, some friends of mine had made a video for a class at Columbine. It was a promotional thing for the play we were doing, *Get Smart*. And the promo had to do with this evil guy blowing up the school.

In the video, the guy points a milk carton at the school and fires a laser out of it. It was over-the-top. It was funny. No one could have possibly taken it seriously. But in the wake of the Columbine massacre, people were looking for anything that might look suspicious; because the guy in the video was wearing a black trench coat, it was immediately assumed that Eric and Dylan must have modeled themselves after it.

So *Inside Edition* showed up at my door, and said that they had a copy of the video. "Do you know anything about it?" they asked.

"Well, yeah," I said.

"Did you help to direct it?"

"No," I replied. "I didn't have anything to do with it. I've just seen it."

They seemed disappointed. "Oh. Well, we're looking for someone who did make this video who will talk to us. Because we're pretty sure that Eric and Dylan saw this video, and that was what inspired them."

Then I got worried. One of the guys who had made that video was Scott Fuselier. His father Dwayne was part of the FBI's Columbine investigation team. *Inside Edition* didn't know that yet, but they would figure it out before too long.

I liked Scott and his dad a great deal. "If this comes out," I thought, "Scott's dad will be absolutely crucified."

So I lied. I said, "Well, now that you mention it, yeah, I did help to make it a little bit." It was bullshit, sure, and lots of people have told me I shouldn't have said it. But in my mind, it was a choice between watching Scott and his dad getting completely screwed—along with everyone else who had been involved in making the video—or trying to take the blame for them. After all, for me, it was no big deal. But, I thought, if *Inside Edition* reported that this FBI investigator's son had made a video that inspired the killers, their lives would be over.

Of course, I didn't stop the media from figuring out who had made the video, and questions were raised, but fortunately Dwayne Fuselier remained on the case. Scott thought I was just clamoring for attention. I've never been able to tell him the real reasons for what I did.

In those early days after Columbine, the people who had been friends with Eric and Dylan stuck together, mainly because the rest of the world hated us. In the same way that people wanted the book thrown at Mark Manes and Philip Duran, our community made us guilty by association. Losing our friends was difficult enough as it was. Imagine listening to your classmates whisper that you were in on it, too.

We didn't really hang out. But when we'd see each other around, we'd feel a mutual respect, just for getting through it all. Often we wouldn't say anything to each other. Just a look, or a nod, was all we needed.

We were torn by conflicting emotions. On the one hand, Eric and Dylan had been our friends. They were dead. They were gone. On the other hand, they had killed thirteen other people. People we had been close to. We had to make a decision: How should we grieve?

Many were struggling with that question. Crosses were erected on Rebel Hill, overlooking the school, that represented each of the lives lost: fifteen crosses in all. Those who put them up wanted to recognize that Eric and Dylan were victims too, even if they were victims of themselves.

Several parents found this objectionable. Brian Rohrbough, who had lost his son Danny that day, was so infuriated that he climbed Rebel Hill and posted signs on the crosses that read "Unrepentant Murderer." After asking the police to remove the crosses and getting nowhere, Rohrbough enlisted the help of a few other parents and took them down himself, cutting them into tiny pieces and destroying them.

At first I was angry about that. The crosses weren't put there to honor Eric and Dylan; people were just paying their respects to the dead. However, looking back on it, I respect what Brian and the parents of the other victims were going through, too. Their sons had been murdered, and Eric and Dylan were responsible. For them, the situation was about as black and white as you can get. I realize now that crosses for Eric and Dylan should have been erected in a spot far away from those of their victims.

People ask me all the time whether Eric and Dylan should be forgiven for what they did. My response is absolutely not. Those two killed people. It doesn't get worse than that.

Will I always remember the good times with them? Absolutely. I'll always remember the bad times, too. They were my friends, and nothing will change that. But as far as forgiveness goes, that's not something I am prepared to do. What they deserve is remembrance. Not forgiveness. There's a difference.

15

I stand accused

SHORTLY AFTER THE COLUMBINE MASSACRE, A MEMORIAL SERVICE was held at Red Rocks Amphitheater on the north side of Denver. Our choir would be singing there, which meant this would be my first official school function since the shooting. I didn't want to go, but my parents convinced me that it would be good for me to see everybody again.

I arrived at the theater and went around backstage to sit with my friends in choir. That was the first time I heard it.

People were whispering about me.

This was different from Rachel's funeral, where people hadn't wanted anything to do with anyone who'd been friends with Eric and Dylan. These people were talking about me specifically. I heard the word "murderer" being thrown around.

There had been rumblings before. Through the grapevine, my brother had learned that at Matt Kechter's funeral, a few of the football players had been talking about getting together and coming after me. I figured they were just talking in the heat of the moment, so I didn't worry too much about it. But this was the first time I had heard people actually suggesting that I had somehow been in on what had happened.

No one said anything to my face. But as I sat there, I could hear whispers behind me. My name. Eric and Dylan. Questions. Suggestions that I knew something.

I tried to shut it out.

Standing in front of us on the stage, Principal DeAngelis told the crowd that there was so much love at Columbine, that we would get through this together. At the same time, I heard it behind me:

"Brooks is a murderer."

The whispers were no longer conversational. They were directed at me. I was supposed to overhear them. And I didn't know what to say or do in response.

By the time superintendent Jane Hammond started her speech, I couldn't take it. I knew I was on the stage, in full view of everyone, but I didn't care. I stood up and left.

Less than two weeks after the shooting, my family got a call from the Columbine school counselor, Mr. Collins. Everyone was gearing up to head for Chatfield High School and finish out the year. The plan was that Columbine students would attend for one half of the day, and Chatfield students would attend for the other half. However, there were some people who wouldn't be welcome at any time.

"We believe it would be in Brooks's best interest not to return to school," Collins told us on our answering machine.

My mom called back, demanding to know why. When she finally got through to Collins, he wouldn't clarify the school's wishes. He kept repeating, simply, "We just think it would be in Brooks's best interest not to return."

I wasn't the only one to get that message. There were over a dozen kids, all friends of Eric and Dylan, who were asked not to return. Most of them took the advice.

I was ready to go back. However, to put it bluntly, the school made me an offer I couldn't refuse. They told me that if I agreed not to return, I would still graduate with passing grades in all of my classes.

I was failing a couple of classes at the time. To be guaranteed passing grades and a diploma, simply for staying at home—it just seemed to make more sense to accept the offer.

That's not to say that I never went back. Once classes started, I made a brief visit to Chatfield. I needed to see my friends again. When I walked in, the police, who were standing guard at the time, paid close attention to me.

The police had been interviewing Eric and Dylan's friends at length ever since the shooting. Sheriff John Stone was convinced that two kids could not have brought in by themselves the sheer amount of explosives found at the scene. There must have been accomplices, he kept telling the press, and that's why the police were talking to all of Eric and Dylan's associates.

I'd already been visited by detectives before I went to Chatfield. They kept asking about Eric's last words to me outside the school. They wanted to know what had made me walk away. At the time, I thought it was because they were trying to reconstruct Eric's movements. As I would later learn, their motives were much more complex

My classmates knew that the police were interviewing guys like Nate and Zach and me. So it was assumed that we must be suspects. After all, if we were friends with Eric and Dylan, then we must have known that the attack was coming, right? Never mind that my little brother was shot at in the cafeteria. Never mind that Eric had threatened to kill me only a year before. As friends of the killers, some people's logic ran, we must have been killers, too.

Maybe I should have thought about that before I went to Chatfield, but at the time I just didn't care. I walked in, ignoring the cops who were watching me. The guard gave me a visitor's badge and a bumper sticker with "We Are Columbine" written on it. Then I was given a two-officer escort to walk around the school.

Not only was the escort incredibly demeaning, but it reinforced the impression that I was guilty in some way in the minds of those who already suspected me. I was just digging my hole deeper. I didn't care at the time; I just wanted to see my friends. In retrospect, though, I shouldn't have gone through with it.

I didn't stay long. People didn't really talk to me. Kids I had called my friends were looking at me funny now. They didn't want me there.

In Littleton, I was making enemies left and right. But in the national media, the reporters just kept coming. I was doing interviews all over the place, from Fox News to the *Today Show* to Tom Brokaw. I would talk to three, sometimes four reporters a day.

Yet I never once did an interview for money. I never sold videotape footage of Eric or Dylan, like one of my classmates did. I wasn't looking to be famous. I just wanted people to understand what had happened, so I accepted a lot of interview requests.

There were two things that my family wanted people to understand: first, that there had been clear warning signs beforehand, and second, that Columbine High School was a much worse place than everyone was letting on.

We were telling people the truth, and we were resented for it.

The police were already under the microscope as it was. They were being criticized for not responding quickly enough to the shootings, making high estimates of the dead before any numbers were released, leaving the bodies in the school overnight, taking too long to reach the wounded, and leaving parents to learn about their children's murders in the newspaper instead of calling them to tell them. So they were playing the game of damage control right from the start, trying to make people believe that there was no way they could have seen this coming, that no one knew how deal with it, that there had been no warning.

Now from out of the blue comes this Brooks Brown kid, talking about some report he filed a year ago about Eric Harris threatening his life and building pipe bombs and vandalizing his neighborhood.

They knew I wasn't lying. They knew the media was listening to me, and the pressure on them was increasing. If they were to keep my story out of the spotlight, they had to discredit my family, and fast.

Sheriff Stone found a way.

I was with my parents when the call came. NBC reporter Dan Abrams told us he had just conducted an interview with Sheriff Stone and wanted to give us a chance to respond before it aired. Within hours, we were sitting with Abrams in front of a TV monitor.

"I'm convinced there are more people involved," Stone had told NBC. "Brooks Brown could be a possible suspect. Mr. Brown, as well as several others, are in the investigative mode."

When Abrams inquired about Eric's Web pages, Stone dismissed them as a "subtle threat," nothing more. Such things wouldn't have been prosecutable, he said. He also dismissed my parents' claims of having reported them in the first place, asking why my parents would have "allowed" me to be friends with Eric Harris if they thought he was dangerous enough to report to police.

"Why did Eric Harris warn Mr. Brown to leave the school on the day he was starting all the shooting?" he said. "Is this a smoke screen?"

My parents were furious. My dad lashed out at the sheriff, saying if anyone was trying to create a smoke screen, it was him.

"He should be ashamed of himself," my dad said of Stone. "They're looking for a scapegoat. They're going to get sued and they know it, and they're looking for someone to blame it on."

As for me, I sat there in complete disbelief, staring at that image of Sheriff Stone on the TV. I didn't know what to say.

Stone's allegations first appeared on NBC, but it didn't take long for them to appear in other media outlets. Shortly after his television appearance, the Jefferson County sheriff repeated his suspicions to USA TODAY.

"I believe Mr. Brown knows a lot more than he has been willing to share with us," Stone told the newspaper. "He's had a long-term involvement with Harris and Klebold, and he was the only student warned to stay away from the school on the day of the shooting."

On May 6, the Denver Post *reiterated Stone's claim that Brooks was a "possible suspect" and that Brooks's statements had been "inconsistent."*

Stone offered no evidence to back this assertion during his interviews, although Jefferson County Undersheriff John Dunaway offered an explanation to Westword *reporter Alan Prendergast nearly a year later. According to the article, Dunaway claimed there were "plenty of reasons" to suspect Brooks.*

"This Brown person is telling us that he is in direct personal contact with Harris moments before the killings begin," Dunaway told Westword. "And Harris tells him that he likes him and that he should leave the school. Then he shows up in a class photo with Harris and Klebold, and they're all pointing fingers at the camera, as if they had guns."

The comment was a reference to the "goofy" class photo that the Columbine High School class of 1999 had posed for. Yet, in Dunaway's eyes, this sort of evidence perfectly justified Stone's remarks to the media.

If Stone's comments were an attempt to discredit the Brown family—as they believe—then it was an extremely effective ploy. It wouldn't take long for Brooks to learn just how much damage the sheriff had caused.

Reporters showed up at my house soon after that first broadcast. They wanted to know my response.

I reiterated my parents' claim that the accusation was just a smoke screen. I reminded reporters that there was no evidence against me. I said that neither the FBI nor the district attorney was calling me a suspect. I said Stone was making himself look bad.

That was my public face. Away from the cameras, Stone's words were destroying my life.

There were already people at school who believed I had something to do with the killing, just because I had been friends with Eric and Dylan. Now people in the community were questioning my innocence, too. People who had been undecided, or who had known nothing about me before, suddenly saw me as "that guy who the police think was in on it."

Shortly after the NBC report, I was walking through a parking lot with Trevor Dolac when a girl leaned out the window of her car and started shouting at me.

"You fucking murderer!" she yelled. "Get the hell out of here!"

Once I was at a stoplight when a car full of Columbine students pulled up next to me and started screaming "Killer!"

Others didn't call me names, but still kept their distance. One night I was with my cousin at the drive-through window of Dairy Queen. It was fairly late, and there weren't any other customers in line. When I pulled up, the employee at the window took one look at me and his eyes got real wide.

He gave us our order without saying another word to me. As we were pulling away, I saw him go to the doors and lock them. He stood there staring at us until we drove away.

Those sorts of things started happening with more frequency as the days progressed. I'd be walking along and hear "asshole" or "killer" yelled at me from passing cars. After a while, I learned to tune it out.

I was having trouble sleeping. I was having trouble eating. I wondered if at some point Stone would move this witch hunt to the next level and have me arrested.

I felt helpless.

The police were pressuring me to take a lie-detector test about my involvement in Columbine. I would have been willing, except that people around me immediately advised against it. A lie detector is a sensitive piece of equipment. Administrators of the test wrap a sensor around your chest to time your breathing. They put pulse sensors on each finger. They look for places where your heart skips a beat during a response, or your breathing becomes shallow, to determine whether you're lying.

My family still feared that the police were trying to put the blame on me, and didn't trust them to administer the test fairly. If I took the test, and their administrator made any adjustments to the machine to make me fail or even seem evasive, it would ruin me.

My aunt, an attorney in Michigan, was the first person to advise me of this. Friends weighed in on the subject as well. Their consensus, based on what had happened so far, was that the police couldn't be trusted.

Nonetheless, I wanted to clear my name, and by not taking a lie detector test, I looked like I had something to hide. So my family came up with a compromise. We paid to have an independent third party conduct the test.

Alverson & Associates, a polygraph company based in Denver, agreed to our request. On May 11, administrator David Henigsman hooked me up to the sensors and began asking questions. He started with simple things, like "Is your name Brooks Brown?" and "Are you a student at Columbine High School?" Then he began asking me about the attack.

He asked if I had ever seen Eric and Dylan's pipe bombs, or if I had ever helped to make one. He asked if I had any prior knowledge of what was going to happen. He asked whether I had any reason to lie.

I passed.

We gave the police the results, including a signed statement from Alverson that I had been truthful. The police weren't satisfied. They wanted the video of the test, the complete transcript, and all computer data. We refused. My dad told them, "Look, Alverson is a trusted name that has been used all over the country. If this isn't going to convince you, then nothing will. We don't owe you anything else at this point."

Even though Stone had named me as a possible suspect, my room was never searched. Neither was my car. My computer wasn't seized. These steps were taken with other acquaintances of Eric and Dylan, even though their names were never given to the press as possible suspects. They weren't with me.

Around the middle of May, my parents got a phone call from the producers of *The Oprah Winfrey Show*. Oprah had already done one show about Columbine, where she had spoken with parents of the victims. Now she wanted to hear from me about what had happened with Eric's Web pages.

My mom turned down the invitation at first; she didn't want people to think we were using the tragedy to meet Oprah Winfrey or to get famous.

The problem was, several media outlets had stopped listening to us about Eric's Web pages. Since the police were denying that we had talked with them, and Stone was suggesting that I'd been in on the attack, they weren't believing my family anymore. We realized that this show was a chance to get our story out there. So, after further consideration, we agreed.

We didn't care about being on TV. We just wanted to get the truth out. We wanted people to know that if something like this could happen at Columbine, it could happen anywhere. All around, we were hearing that music had caused Columbine, or video games had caused Columbine. We had to counter that.

People needed to know that bullying and injustice had caused this. Parents and administrators not being attentive to the needs of their kids had caused this. We didn't want anyone else to go through what our community had suffered. We wanted to help stop Columbine from happening again.

I also had the opportunity to speak up in my defense, to answer the accusations before a national audience.

We appeared on the show May 21. Oprah's producers provided the tickets to Chicago, where the show is taped. I was actually nervous about getting on a plane; I've always hated flying. Nonetheless, after the events of the past month, leaving Littleton behind for a little while was a relief.

It was hard to make it through the taping. Only a few days before, I had finally come to grips with the idea that Eric and Dylan really were dead, that I would never be able to confront them with what they had done, would never have that outlet for my pain and confusion. It had only been a month since the shootings; my emotions were still raw.

I thought I was prepared to talk, but then the taping began. Immediately the producers played a "montage" tape that showed our community in mourning, video footage of Dylan, and a general review of the events of April 20. At the end, Oprah projected the drawing I'd made when Dylan and I were in grade school. It showed two friends holding hands, with a caption underneath that said, "What scares me most is if Dylan does boast that he isn't my friend."

Seeing it all projected up there, I felt all the pain coming back. It was all I could do not to start crying all over again. And it was right at that moment that the video ended and the lights came up on me.

"Brooks still cannot believe his boyhood friend has done this," Oprah said, turning to me.

I nodded, and took a breath.

"And I know that the Klebolds, if they had known about Eric's Web page, if they had known anything about any of this—they would have been all over it," I said.

My mom went on to explain how we had turned over the Web pages, and the police hadn't followed up on them. My dad told Oprah about the different options the police could have pursued. I talked about my last conversation with Eric, the atmosphere of the school, and how I was still trying to understand what had happened.

We were joined during the show by Gavin DeBecker, an expert on predicting violence and author of the book *Protecting the Gift: Keeping Children and Teenagers Safe*. DeBecker was quick to criticize Sheriff Stone for his comments.

"I think what the sheriff's comments about Brooks seemed to indicate, when he said he may be a suspect, is that typical example of institutional BS that says 'those people know something about our department, and I want to now reduce their credibility,' " DeBecker said.

Instead of finding the easiest ways to point fingers and avoid blame, DeBecker said, people need to look deeper for the answers. He suggested that kids in my generation had "grown up with death in a way that you and I never did."

"This is their world," he said. "These boys give us all the opportunity to look at ourselves.... The shooting gives us the opportunity to say, 'Hey, what's this about?' Something's clearly different here when boys are going into high schools and doing this. We have an opportunity now."

Oprah encouraged people to learn from what had happened at Columbine.

"I'm thinking if we don't learn from this, we'll see it again," she said.

Those words echoed my own feelings. Since we had been denied the chance to ask Eric and Dylan why they had done what they'd done, we would have to learn on our own.

My family's appearance on *The Oprah Winfrey Show* helped get the word out. Other shows invited us to appear as well. However, one particular appearance wound up falling through.

I had been invited to participate in a group talk with President Bill Clinton in early June. The discussion, called "Kids and Guns," would have Clinton presiding over a panel of teens from around the country. It would be televised on ABC's *Good Morning America.*

The night before I was going to get on a plane for Washington, D.C., the network called to rescind my invitation. I had been removed because as "a witness in an active investigation," I would not be allowed to enter the White House. A different student from Columbine wound up attending in my place.

When they told me that, I just laughed. That was all I could do.

The day after our appearance on *The Oprah Winfrey Show* aired, graduation ceremonies were held for the Class of 1999. We tried to make it seem as normal as possible. My family posed for photos with me in my robe before we left for the ceremony. My parents told me how proud they were.

Still, there was no getting past the shadow that hung over that day. The ceremony was being televised nationally. Everyone was watching us.

Principal DeAngelis gave a speech to the 437 kids that were graduating that day.

"Two of the graduating seniors of the Class of 1999 and one of the faculty members are no longer with us," he said. "Their lives were cut down too short. Their lives were full of courage and hope and enthusiasm. We will never forget that they loved us as much as we loved them. Each of us will carry the spirit of Isaiah Shoels, Lauren Townsend, and Dave Sanders into the future."

Valeen Schnurr, Jeanna Park, and Lisa Kreutz, all of whom had been wounded at Columbine, were there to receive their diplomas. Lauren Townsend's family walked across the stage to accept her diploma.

I felt drained afterwards. My parents gave me a hug, and then I stepped away for a moment, to be alone with my thoughts. When I did so, I became aware of someone standing behind me. It was Principal DeAngelis.

I hadn't spoken to him since the shootings.

"How are you, Brooks?" he asked.

I shrugged. "I'm doing." Seeing as how the administration had asked me not to return to school, I really didn't feel like talking to him.

"What did you think of my speech?" he asked.

I paused and looked at him.

"I thought it was bad," I said after a moment.

DeAngelis looked taken aback. "What?"

"Look, fifteen people died that day," I said. "Not just the kids that you named up there. We lost people that day that you didn't even count. That your school cost the lives of. Avoiding the truth doesn't change it."

"I just thought it would make it nicer for these kids," DeAngelis said. "Easier to deal with."

"You're wrong," I said. I turned and walked away.

DeAngelis followed me. He'd been reading the papers; he knew my family had been speaking out against the atmosphere at Columbine. "What did I do?" he asked me. "Why are you and your parents so upset with me?"

I could have told him. For four years, the administration had turned a blind eye to the torment the unpopular kids suffered every day. They had allowed that atmosphere of hate and cruelty to exist. And now—even as DeAngelis gave speech after speech about Columbine being "full of love"—the school had asked me and the rest of Eric and Dylan's friends to just "go away" after the shootings. The words he had said to the cameras did not reflect reality.

I didn't feel like fighting with him about it, though. Graduation was over. I was done with that school now.

I walked away from DeAngelis and rejoined my family.

At the same time students were graduating from Columbine, Sheriff Stone told the Denver Post *he was "bowing out of the media maelstrom."*

Stone's accusation against Brooks wasn't the only thing he'd done that was attracting criticism. From the beginning, Stone made blunders and comments to the media that were either uninformed or flat-out incorrect.

On the day of the shooting, Stone said there were "up to twenty-five dead," even though parents were still at Leawood Elementary waiting for word on their children. Stone claimed that Eric and Dylan tried three times to escape the school and were turned back by gunfire each time. The official report from the sheriff's office later indicated that no such thing had happened.

Early in the investigation, Stone spoke about how he believed the parents of Eric and Dylan should be held accountable. Those words might have scared off the Harrises from cooperating with investigators; they demanded immunity from prosecution before they would consent to police interviews, and when that immunity was denied, they refused to talk.

He also implied that three students who were detained outside of the school on the day of the shooting might be involved. The three students identified themselves as the "Splatter Punks." They said they were only there because they had heard about the shootings on the radio and come to the school out of curiosity.

Stone told authorities he suspected them "because the shootings were not on the radio at that time." Yet his department's own official spokesman pointed out that the students had already been cleared. Stone wound up holding a midnight press conference to tell reporters that what he'd said earlier that day was wrong.

In a May 7, 1999 article, "Colorado Sheriff to Stop Talking to Reporters," Washington Post writer Tom Kenworthy shared concerns from local authorities about Sheriff Stone.

"To some senior law enforcement officials here, none of whom will comment publicly, Stone is violating a cardinal rule of criminal investigations: Don't say anything that might tip off possible subjects or potentially jeopardize future prosecutions," Kenworthy wrote. "Stone's sometimes ill-considered public statements, they suggest, reflect his lack of senior law enforcement experience and training, and underscore how far removed he is now from his days as a policeman in suburban Lakewood."

By the time I graduated, the Jefferson County Sheriff's Department had already conducted three interviews with me. So it wasn't a surprise to my mom when they called again in July for another conversation.

The police said they had my backpack. When we got back to my house on April 20 and I saw my brother run out of the house, I jumped out of the car and ran to hug him; I left my backpack behind. It had never occurred to me to go back for it, so it had remained in Ryan Schwayder's backseat.

On May 18, Detective Jon Watson interviewed Ryan about what had happened. Watson asked at length about my actions that day; Ryan explained that he and Deanna had picked me up, and I had told them there was a shooting. According to Watson's report, Ryan's mom commented that my bag was still in the Jeep. Watson chose to take it.

Over those next two months, the police went through the contents of my backpack, looking for something that would connect me to Columbine. Now they were calling my parents for a fourth interview—and they had a "revelation" in store.

When she answered the phone, Judy Brown said, the officer on the other end was very polite and friendly. He said the police had Brooks's backpack, and that they were going to bring it over to the house.

"You don't have to do that," she said. "We'll come down and get it."

"No, no," the officer replied. "I want to do this for you, because I'm sure you and Mr. Brown have questions for me, and we want to answer every question you have."

"Okay, then," Judy said. "Just drop on by."

"No, I want to make an appointment," the officer said. "And you're sure Mr. Brown will be there, too?"

That seemed like an odd request to Judy, if the officers were simply bringing a book bag over. Later that day, two officers sat down at her kitchen table and pulled out several of Brooks's notebooks. They had looks of "grave concern" on their faces, Judy said.

"We have some things that are really going to upset you, Mr. and Mrs. Brown," they told Randy.

The other leaned in close. "We think you're in danger."

I came home in time to see my parents at the table with the police. At first it didn't strike me as anything unusual; we'd had so many conversations with the police and the FBI that it had become common to see them around. However, I quickly noticed that this time, they were being a lot more confrontational than before.

They had one of my old notebooks, with my poem about Robert Craig in it. I had written that poem the year before, shortly after Robert had committed suicide. The poem was from Robert's point of view; it talked about depression and death, and his desire to murder his father. The police had read the poem and interpreted it to mean that I was plotting against my own parents.

Trying to keep my cool, I pointed out that underneath the poem, I had written "Dedicated to Robert Craig." They asked me about other poems in my notebook that also dealt with dark subjects. "Look, I write a lot, and it isn't happy all the time," I said.

The police had pages of song lyrics that I had printed out from my computer. The police believed I had written them myself, and that they were all about anger and killing. I took one look at them and immediately pointed out which Insane Clown Posse album they were from. Anyone with knowledge of contemporary music or computers would have recognized that the lyrics had been printed from the Internet. These police officers, however, didn't understand that.

The police pulled out "eyewitness reports" suggesting that I had known about Eric's pipe bombs. One lady had told them she "saw my white car parked over at Eric's house all the time." My parents pointed out that I don't have a white car.

Next, they had a neighbor who said he'd been jogging one evening when he saw Eric and me together. According to this witness, I was on a red bike, wearing a black trench coat, and Eric and I were "lighting something."

I don't own a black trench coat, nor do I have a red bike. "Go ahead and look in our garage," my mom said. "See if there's a red bike there."

My parents asked when this "incident" had supposedly happened.

"It was around March or April of 1998," the officer replied.

My parents argued that at that time Eric and I had not even been speaking. In fact, Eric had wanted me dead and posted threats against me. My parents reminded the investigators about Eric's Web pages.

"We're not here to talk about that," the officers replied.

The interview went on for three hours. They kept repeating, "We want Brooks to take another lie detector test. We want our own test." Even though we had rebuttals for every piece of "evidence" they pulled out of my bag, they weren't backing down.

Finally my dad said, "You know what? This interview is over. Don't come back unless you really have something."

The officers left. They had come to prove to my parents that I was a killer, and left looking like fools. Nonetheless, the fact that this had happened almost three months after Stone's original accusation showed that the sheriff wasn't letting up.

16

the families

A QUESTION I STRUGGLED WITH IN THE MONTHS AFTER THE ATTACK was how to deal with the families of the victims. On the one hand, I wanted to be able to extend my sympathies to them. On the other, I knew they were being fed information from the police that I'd been involved. Because of that, I never knew how to approach them.

I didn't always know when I was going to run into them. One time, I was spending the day with Kevin Larson, who had been the lead singer of our band the summer before. He had started dating a girl named Erin Fleming. The two of us went over to her house; as I was sitting in her living room, I looked around and noticed pictures all over the walls of Kelly Fleming, who had died in the Columbine library. Shaken, I realized that Erin Fleming was Kelly's sister.

I spoke to her mother briefly, telling her who I was and how I knew Erin. We didn't talk about Kelly at all. To be honest, once I had made the connection, I felt really uncomfortable being there. Her parents were very nice, but it was an awkward situation.

I tried to e-mail Tom Mauser a few times. Since I had mentored his son Danny on the debate team, I felt like I should say something now that Danny was gone. Mr. Mauser never wrote me back.

I understand what must have been going through his mind, considering what the sheriff was saying about me. Still, it's hard when you want to tell a dad how special you thought his kid was, and you can't, because he's been told that you had something to do with his son's death.

Like many of the other parents, Rich Petrone, Daniel Rohrbough's stepfather, wasn't sure what to think about me. But my dad, who knew Rich from the real estate business, managed to talk with him, explaining that the Web pages we had reported to the media were real, and that we were willing to share them. In fact, he said, we were willing to share anything they wanted to see.

This was important, because the deadline for filing lawsuits over the shootings was approaching. Mr. Petrone knew that if we could prove we had reported Eric's Web pages to the police, it would show that the police had had prior warning. So Mr. Petrone arranged for us to meet with Daniel's father, Brian Rohrbough.

Brian Rohrbough has never settled for easy answers. From the moment his son Danny was killed at Columbine, he demanded information from the police about what had happened and why.

Danny had been killed on the steps outside Columbine High School. He was clearly visible in helicopter footage from TV news reports; the next day, his parents saw a giant photo of his body in the newspaper. It was the first real confirmation they'd had of his death; no one from the sheriff's office had notified them. In fact, Danny's body wasn't moved from that sidewalk for well over a day. The police claimed there were fears of the bodies being "booby-trapped," and that's why they were left on the ground for so long. Rich Petrone had even offered to sign a waiver saying he didn't care if he got blown up, "but he wasn't going to let Danny's body stay on that sidewalk for another day."

In the first few months of the investigation, Rohrbough sought constant updates on any conspirators in the attack.

"While I wasn't jumping to any conclusions, I was trying to learn about all of Harris and Klebold's acquaintances," he says. "I had heard the sheriff say Brooks Brown was a suspect. And at the time, I had no reason to not believe what police were saying."

Six weeks after Stone's comments about Brooks, Rohrbough went to the sheriff and asked what was going on. "I said to him, 'You told me this Brown kid was a suspect. When are you going to arrest him?' " he recalls. "Stone told me that Brooks wasn't involved. I didn't think much about that until later, when I realized, 'Wait a minute. The sheriff told me he's not involved, yet his name is still being thrown around in public.' That was when I first realized that there was something wrong.

"Even so, I still honestly didn't know what was going on," he said. "I wasn't jumping to any conclusions. I was just waiting for evidence."

Now, months later, the Petrones had arranged a meeting between Rohrbough and Brooks's parents. The meeting would take place at the Petrones' home.

"It was very uncomfortable when we first walked in," Judy Brown recalls. Brian had not arrived yet, and there was a period of tension while they waited with Sue Petrone, Danny Rohrbough's mother. However, once Rohrbough arrived, the Browns started showing the families printouts of Eric's Web pages. Rohrbough was stunned by what he saw.

"Many of the people who tried to offer help didn't have any information I could use," he says. "They'd heard something from their neighbor, or something like that, and there would be no way to confirm it. When I met with the Browns, though, it was interesting—because not only did they know something, they had documentation. They gave me close to two hundred pages of Web printouts, transcripts, and handwritten notes. There was definitely something there."

The Browns carefully explained their history with Eric Harris, and the report they had made to the police the year before.

"You could see the confusion," Judy Brown recalls. "And then, in Brian's face, you could see it hit him: 'Oh, my God, the police have been lying to us about this.' "

Rohrbough was amazed to learn that the police had never taken Brooks's computer. They had never searched his house. They had never searched his car. They hadn't even questioned him until six days after the attack. "If he's such a big suspect, why didn't they investigate him?" he asked.

Judy Brown made Rohrbough an offer. If he wanted, he could be alone in a room with Brooks—no attorneys, no family members to interfere—and ask him anything. The offer impressed Rohrbough.

"From a parent's point of view, that would be one of the first things you would offer if your son has nothing to hide," Rohrbough said.

However, Rich Petrone made another suggestion: perhaps it would be better for Brooks to show Rohrbough in person where he was on the day of the attack. The families agreed to meet at Columbine High School, to walk the route Brooks had taken that day.

I was scared to meet Brian. I really was. My friends had been responsible for Danny Rohrbough's death. I felt so ashamed of that, and I didn't know what his father, who had been angry enough to tear down the memorial crosses that had been erected for Eric and Dylan, would say to me. On top of that, it would be the first time I'd ever retraced my steps from April 20. I didn't know what to expect.

My parents went with me to Columbine, where we met the Petrones and the Rohrboughs. I thought I had steeled myself for anything; I didn't know if Danny's parents would be rude to me, or if they believed I was to blame. What I hadn't expected was my own reaction when I saw Mr. Rohrbough for the first time. I started to cry.

"He looks like his son," I said to my mom.

I led the group over to the spot where I'd seen Eric pull into the parking lot. From there, we walked down Pierce, where I heard the first shots. I explained that they had sounded like nail guns, and Brian nodded. Brian was asking questions the entire way, wanting to know what I did at each point along the way. I didn't know it at the time, but he was timing us as we walked. He wanted to make sure my account matched up with everything else he'd heard.

After we had finished the walk, I was badly in need of a cigarette. I shook his hand and stepped away so he could talk to my parents.

In a way, it felt good to talk with one of the victims' parents at length. Now they knew me as a person, rather than just a name they'd heard from the police. At the same time, though, I just felt overwhelmed, especially after taking that walk again. It made the memories way too fresh.

While the walk had been difficult, it was helpful for Brian Rohrbough to finally receive a firsthand account of that day's events. Also, Brooks's explanation matched what Rohrbough had already learned. Matt Houck, who had been in the backseat of Ryan Schwayder's car when Brooks called 911, had also talked to Rohrbough about what had happened that day.

"What Brooks was saying fit the scenario, it fit the surroundings, and it fit what we had already heard from other people," Rohrbough says. "At the time, there wasn't much information available, so you never knew what to believe. But when you get stories that start to match, there's a much greater chance that they're right."

Today, Rohrbough believes Brooks was being used by the police.

"It became pretty obvious that Brooks was a convenient person to blame, because of what his father was saying [about the Web pages],"

Rohrbough said. "The easiest way to shut his dad up was to say, 'Well, he's trying to protect his kid, because his kid's involved.' And that's what most of the press believed. I sat in on a meeting with a group of reporters who were talking about how mad they were, because they believed what the sheriff was telling them off the record ... Clearly, the easiest way to shut up somebody is to go after their kid. And that's what the police were doing."

The Rohrboughs and the Petrones were the first parents that I had the chance to talk extensively with. Later, I received a call from Darrell Scott, Rachel Scott's father.

Mr. Scott had already co-authored a book about his daughter, entitled *Rachel's Tears*. Now he was putting together a tribute video, made up of comments from people who had known her. He had a photo of me studying with Rachel before a debate competition, and he knew that she and I had been friends. So he asked me to participate.

I agreed. I wanted to do it for Rachel.

Mr. Scott and I went to Clement Park, and when he turned on the camera I just started talking. I said that if Eric and Dylan had thought they were getting back at all the people who had made fun of them, they had made a horrible mistake by killing Rachel. If there was one person who would have accepted them, it was her. I talked about our first discussion on faith. I wanted to make it clear that Rachel had never judged people by their beliefs, despite what Bruce Porter had said at her funeral.

Rachel Scott was one of the most beautiful people I've ever known, and being able to speak in her memory gave me one small piece of closure. I thank her family for giving me that chance.

To this day, it's still awkward when I'm around the families of the people Eric and Dylan wounded or killed. No matter how nice they are to me, I know that somewhere deep down, they're looking at me and thinking, "I lost my child to those two sick bastards, and this guy was their friend." It's hard to approach them. It's hard to talk to them.

Still, once I get to talking with them, they understand that I really didn't have any clue about what was going to happen. They realize that I lost people that day, too. I'm not a conspirator. I'm just another person, and the friends I thought I knew betrayed me.

17

the videotapes

ON THE FIRST DAY OF SCHOOL IN THE FALL OF 1999, COLUMBINE HELD
a "Take Back the School" ceremony. It was the first time classes had
resumed at the building since April 20. Repair crews had spent the summer
removing all evidence of Eric and Dylan's rampage. Ceiling tiles were
replaced, water damage from the fire sprinklers was repaired, and bullet
holes and broken glass were removed. A wall of lockers was installed in
front of the entrance to the library, which had been permanently sealed.

Brooks's brother Aaron, a junior, had to return to Columbine. He
remembers the bizarre atmosphere of the first day. Media trucks filled nearby Clement Park. Principal Frank DeAngelis's welcoming speech was carried live by CNN. Parents stood side by side in front of the entrance to shield
students from the media as they entered the school.

Once inside, though—where cameras were banned—things were more
subdued.

"Things were better at Columbine, as far as how people treated one
another," Aaron recalls. "At least, that's how it was for the first month or so.
But by two or three months after we got back, things were back to the way
they had been before. The name-calling started up all over again. Some people had changed a lot, but others hadn't changed at all."

❖

I was worried about my brother when he went back into that school. Principal DeAngelis repeatedly denied to the media that he saw any bullying going on. He kept making "We Are Columbine" speeches and talking about how the school was coming together. The administration wasn't facing the fact that kids were still as cruel to one another as ever.

Meanwhile, different organizations were using Eric and Dylan to promote their causes. Gun-control advocates arguing for more restrictive gun laws rose up against legal gun owners, starting with a protest outside the National Rifle Association's convention in Denver shortly after Columbine.

But tougher gun laws wouldn't have stopped Eric and Dylan. They went around one law by using Robyn Anderson to buy weapons at a gun show, and broke another entirely by buying their TEC-9 from a friend. All that gun-control advocates were doing was punishing law-abiding gun owners for Eric and Dylan's misdeeds.

Some tried to say Eric and Dylan were out to kill minorities, because they called Isaiah Shoels a "nigger" and then killed him. It's true Eric posted criticisms of other races on his Web site from time to time, and I have no doubt that they did call Isaiah what they did. However, they also killed twelve other people who were white. It seems clear that racist feelings weren't the motivating force behind the shootings.

Rather, I think Eric and Dylan were determined to humiliate all their victims, no matter who they were. Library witnesses said they made fun of another kid because of his glasses. They said they wanted to kill "anyone with a white hat," because athletes wore white hats. They found some way to mock or degrade each person before they fired the fatal shot. It was one big game to them.

Along the same lines, it doesn't seem that Eric and Dylan specifically targeted people because of their religion. Witnesses remember them asking several people whether they "believed in God" before shooting them. Those stories were repeated throughout the media.

As a result, religious organizations quickly picked up on Columbine. They tried to make people believe the shooting represented a "crisis of faith," that Eric and Dylan had gone into Columbine for the sole purpose of killing as many Christians as possible.

One of the best-known examples they held up is Cassie Bernall, who was killed in the library. More than one witness there claimed that Eric and Dylan asked Cassie if she believed in God, and that when she said yes, she was shot. Her parents wrote a book entitled *She Said Yes: The Unlikely Martyrdom of Cassie Bernall*, which became a bestseller.

However, according to the *Rocky Mountain News*, a student named Emily Wyant—who was crouched down next to Cassie underneath a table—told police that the exchange never happened.

Another library witness, Craig Scott (Rachel's brother), was one of the kids who told police he had heard Cassie say yes. According to a December 14 *Rocky Mountain News* article, "Inside the Columbine Investigation," police took Craig into the library and asked him what direction the question had come from.

"When he revisited the library, he realized the voice had come from another direction—from the table where student Valeen Schnurr had been shot," Dan Luzadder and Kevin Vaughn wrote. "Investigators came to believe it was probably Valeen, who survived, who told the gunmen of her faith in God."

Author P. Solomon Banda of the Associated Press wrote a Dec. 27, 1999 article entitled "Who Said 'Yes' To Columbine Gunmen? Faithful Say It's Immaterial." In the article, Schnurr said she was "blown out from underneath a table by a shotgun blast" from Eric or Dylan.

"One of the gunmen asked her if she believed in God and she said 'yes,' crawling away as he reloaded," Banda wrote.

TIME Magazine shared a different scenario in its Dec. 20, 1999 cover story, "The Columbine Tapes." Author Tim Roche wrote, "When Harris found Cassie Bernall, he leaned down. 'Peekaboo,' he said, and killed her. His shotgun kicked, stunning him and breaking his nose."

Yet even when these doubts surfaced, there were some who said the question was irrelevant. Banda wrote:

> "It doesn't matter who said it or if no one said it," [church volunteer Sara] Evans said. "But if people believe in God, that's what's important."
>
> Doug Clark, director of field ministries of San Diego-based National Network of Youth Ministries, said he encourages other students to follow the teens' example of boldness. "Mincing words over what was said in the library is a minor part," Clark said. "The greater part is how they lived their lives, and it's not going to change anything."
>
> Religious experts said attempts to clarify the confusion sur-rounding the stories of Christian faith actually could help embed the story in religious circles.
>
> "This rethinking can be chalked up to media scrutiny, which I think the faithful would dismiss as a cynical attempt to debunk the story," said Randall Balmer, professor of American Religious Studies at Barnard College. "In some ways, it may make the faithful dig in a little bit deeper and resist those attempts." ("Who Said 'Yes' To Columbine Gunmen?" P. Solomon Banda, Associated Press, 12/27/99)

Balmer's assessment was accurate. On the Web site cassie-bernall.org, Christian author Wendy Murray Zoba posted an article enti-tled "Did She or Didn't She?" with a clear slant against any reporter who questioned the story. She criticized *Salon.com* writer Dave Cullen for airing doubts, writing, "In fact, it is Cullen's piece—and the Jefferson County Sheriff's Department information office—that should be called into account."

Zoba's article showed a clear double standard. On the one hand, she tried to debunk witnesses like Emily Wyant by quoting trauma recovery expert Dee Dee McDermott:

> [McDermott] says, "Some people have a great capacity for processing the trauma and are able to stay, what we call, 'fully present.' They have a high level of recall. Other students are so traumatized, they do not have the capacity to process all the information. Those students would be the ones who would have what we would call memory blocks. A diagnosis for this is Post Traumatic Stress Disorder. There was smoke [in the library] which was disorienting, and they were in study [carrels] with hard wood sides.... People who are interviewing these kids need to understand the dynamics of what trauma does and how they're processing it." ("Did She or Didn't She?" Wendy Murray Zoba, cassiebernall.org.)

In other words, library witnesses like Emily were suffering from "stress disorder" that affected their memory.

On the other hand, witnesses like Craig Scott and Josh Lapp, whom she cited as remembering the exchange, suffered from no such disorientation—except that Scott was "disoriented" when he heard the question come from Valeen Schnurr's direction rather than from Cassie Bernall's. Zoba quoted Craig Scott as saying, "The whole world can say Cassie never said 'yes' to the gunmen, and I'd still stand by my knowledge that she did."

People were turning my high school's tragedy into a tool for their political causes. Zoba was not an objective third party. She was the associate editor for *Christianity Today* and the author of their Oct. 4, 1999 cover story, "Do You Believe In God? How Columbine Changed America." She has written an entire book about faith in regard to Columbine, entitled *Day of Reckoning*.

I'm not claiming that Eric and Dylan didn't have a certain hatred for religion. They did. In fact, we had many discussions about how difficult it could be for a non-Christian at Columbine. Many Littleton residents equate Christianity with being a good person, and they look down on those who are not members of the church. It was hard for Eric and Dylan to watch self-proclaimed "Christians" who pushed other kids around, shoved them into lockers and call them faggots, then got up later and talked about how "important" their faith was. I know for a fact that things like that made Eric and Dylan angry.

Yet, even if it is true that Cassie and Rachel said "yes," it doesn't mean Eric and Dylan's sole intention was to kill Christians. Eleven other people were shot without even being asked the question. Also, there were no stories of kids who said no and were allowed to live.

Zoba concluded her article with the following quote from investigator Gary Muse: "If Cassie's exchange with the gunmen is not germane to the investigation—and I don't believe it is—why are people so interested in debunking the account?"

My answer is simple: It isn't anti-Christian to have questions about Cassie's exchange. It's insulting to suggest that I shouldn't be allowed to seek clarity, in the wake of all the controversy surrounding the story. Cassie was my classmate. I have a right to try to learn the reasons for her death.

By December we would get our first glimpse of those reasons—from Eric and Dylan themselves.

That fall, we learned that *TIME Magazine* was working on an in-depth story about the Columbine investigation. Reporter Tim Roche, who wanted to know more about Eric's Web pages, contacted my family.

Roche conducted several interviews with us at our home. When he came over for the last one, he had a stunned look on his face. "You're not going to believe what the cops just showed me," he said.

Roche had just viewed Eric and Dylan's basement videotapes.

The tapes, which were found by the police in Eric's home on the day of the massacre, had been a well-guarded secret in the months since then. We knew they existed, and the police had read excerpts from them during a sentencing hearing for one of the gun suppliers, but when members of the media and the families of the victims asked to view them, they were denied. Now, however, Roche had seen them.

Apparently his access was very generous. On December 20, 1999, *TIME* printed its exclusive story, "The Columbine Tapes: The Killers Tell Why They Did It." The story featured extensive quotes from the videos, as well as Roche's assessment of them:

> *The tapes were meant to be their final word, to all those who had picked on them over the years, and to everyone who would come up with a theory about their inner demons. It is clear listening to them that Harris and Klebold were not just having trouble with what their counselors called 'anger management.' They fed the anger, fueled it, so the fury could take hold, because they knew they would need it to do what they set out to do. "More rage. More rage," Harris says. "Keep building it on," he says, motioning with his hands for emphasis.*

Harris recalls how he moved around so much with his mili-
tary family and always had to start over, "at the bottom of the
ladder." People continually made fun of him—"my face, my hair,
my shirts." As for Klebold, "If you could see all the anger I've
stored over the past four f—ing years ..." he says.... As far back
as the Foothills Day Care center, he hated the "stuck-up" kids he
felt hated him. "Being shy didn't help," he admits. "I'm going to
kill you all. You've been giving us s— for years." ("The
Columbine Tapes," TIME, 12/20/99)

Sheriff Stone came under heavy criticism for having ignored repeated pleas from the families to see the videotapes but allowed a reporter
from *TIME* to see them. Stone countered by claiming that Roche had
agreed never to quote from them, and had broken the agreement.

TIME denied that any such agreement had ever been entered into.
Roche told my mother that the accusations were not only false, but were
ruining his credibility as a journalist, because now people believed that he
was willing to burn a source for the sake of a story. I knew he would not
have lied about how things happened. He was a great guy, and an honest
reporter. The police were rolling over him to protect themselves—just
like they'd done with me.

Stone made another attempt at damage control. This time, he said he
hadn't yet viewed the tapes himself, so he didn't know what they contained when he gave Roche permission to see them. This was hardly a
good way to avoid criticism; as *Denver Post* columnist Chuck Green
pointed out, "Although he is in charge of the Columbine investigation,
Sheriff Stone hadn't taken the time to sit in a chair and watch the remark-
able videotapes of Harris and Klebold planning the crime."

After it became known that Stone had allowed a reporter to view the
tapes, other members of the media demanded the right to see them as

well. In a last-ditch effort to defuse the situation, Stone proposed two screenings of the videos—one for the media and the other for the families. My parents got wind of this, and they headed over to the sheriff's office to see the tapes for themselves.

Randy and Judy Brown followed the arrows that led them through the Dakota Building, near the Jefferson County Sheriff's Office, until they reached the room where the videos were to be screened. As the tapes were about to begin, the police asked to see press credentials.

"We don't have any," Judy said.

The officer demanded their names. When the Browns told him, he replied that they couldn't be there.

"Yes, we can," Randy replied. "We're citizens and we're going to see those tapes."

"No, you're not," the officer replied.

Randy didn't back down. "Are you going to arrest me if I go in that room?" he asked. Behind the officer, members of the press were watching the exchange with interest.

"No," the officer replied after a moment.

With that, Randy marched past. "Rather than have a knock-down drag-out fight with them, we allowed them in," Deputy Wayne Holverson told Holly Kurtz and Lynn Bartels of the Denver Rocky Mountain News. *"They wanted to watch the tapes, and we figured this was as good a time as any."*

One of the officers spoke with Judy in the hallway while Randy went into the screening room. The officer warned her that the tapes were "extremely disturbing," but he recognized her right to see them.

The officer called detective Kate Battan over to meet Judy. "She was so friendly, and said hello," Judy recalls. "Then the officer said, 'This is

Judy Brown.' Kate just threw her hands in the air and walked away. The officer said, 'Well, I don't know what that was about.' She clearly didn't want to talk to me."

Judy rejoined her husband inside the screening room just as the first tape was beginning. What she saw, she says, horrified her.

Eric and Dylan's basement tapes have never been released for viewing by the general public—at least, as of the writing of this book. However, I've been able to learn a lot about them from what my parents remember seeing, as well as by reading the police summary of their contents (contained in a report released by the sheriff's office in November, 2000). This is what I have been able to put together.

On the first tape, Eric and Dylan are seated in the basement of Eric's house, with Eric holding a shotgun he calls "Arlene," named after a character in *Doom*. Eric is wearing a Rammstein T-shirt with "Wilder Wein"—German for "Wild Wine"—written on it. He and Dylan are drinking a bottle of Jack Daniels as they speak.

At first they talk about weapons. "Thanks to Mark John Doe and Philip John Doe," they say, referring to Mark Manes and Philip Duran, who provided them with their TEC-9. "We used them; they had no clue. If it hadn't been them, it would have been someone else over twenty-one."

Eric tells how close he came to being caught when the Green Mountain Guns store called his house. His father answered, and the clerk said, "Your clips are in." His father replied that he hadn't ordered any clips and left the matter there. Eric laughs as he recounts the story. He also mentions the time when his parents found a pipe bomb but never searched for others. He recalls the time he walked past his mother when his shotgun was "in my terrorist bag sticking out." She thought it was his pellet gun, he says.

The two are still angry about their arrest for the van break-in over a year before. "Fuck you, Walsh," Dylan says, a reference to the officer who caught them.

Eric and Dylan get up to take a tour of Eric's bedroom, "to see all the illegal shit." Eric shows off his stash of weapons; "Thanks to the gun show, and to Robyn," he says. "Robyn is very cool."

Eric then shows off how he's managed to keep his weapons hidden. My mom specifically remembers Eric pulling out a desk drawer filled with clocks of different sizes and shapes, along with batteries and solar igniters, which Eric planned to use for the propane bombs. Eric has pipe bombs hidden behind his CD collection; inside a "Demon Knight" CD is his receipt from Green Mountain Guns for nine ammunition magazines. However, he also has "fifty feet of cannon fuse" hanging on the wall in plain sight.

Eric holds up some of his gear in front of the camera. "What you will find on my body in April," he says.

The two appear in a second video dated March 18, once again seated in the basement. Writers Karen Abbott and Dan Luzadder of the Denver *Rocky Mountain News* viewed the tapes during the media screening and offered the following observation in their December 13, 1999 story, "War Is War":

> They explain over and over why they want to kill as many people as they can. Kids taunted them in elementary school, in middle school, in high school. Adults wouldn't let them strike back, to fight their tormenters, the way such disputes once were settled in schoolyards. So they gritted their teeth. And their rage grew. "It's humanity," Klebold says, flipping an obscene gesture toward the camera. "Look at what you made," he tells the world. "You're fucking shit, you humans, and you deserve to die." ...

They speak at length about all the people who wronged them. "You've given us shit for years," Klebold says. "You're fucking going to pay for all the shit. We don't give a shit because we're going to die doing it." ("War Is War," *Rocky Mountain News,* 12/13/99)

Dylan asks Eric if he thinks the cops will listen to the entire video. Eric replies that he believes the cops will chop the video up into little pieces, "and the police will just show the public what they want it to look like." They suggest delivering the videos to TV stations right before the attack. After all, they want people to know that they feel they have their reasons.

"We are but aren't psycho," they say.

On another tape, at Dylan's house, Eric videotapes Dylan trying on his weapons. Dylan is wearing a black T-shirt with "Wrath" written on it—the same shirt he would wear on the day of the attack.

Dylan promises his parents that there was nothing they could have done to stop him. According to the *Rocky Mountain News* article "War Is War," "You can't understand what we feel," he says. "You can't understand, no matter how much you think you can."

The *Rocky Mountain News* quoted Eric as offering praise for his parents. "My parents are the best fucking parents I have ever known," he says. "My dad is great. I wish I was a fucking sociopath so I don't have any remorse, but I do. This is going to tear them apart. They will never forget it."

According to police reports, Eric expresses regret on another tape as well. He recorded one segment while driving alone in his car. "It's a weird feeling, knowing you're going to be dead in two and a half weeks," he says to the camera. He talks about the co-workers he will miss, and says he wishes he could have revisited Michigan and "old friends." The officer who viewed this tape wrote that "at this point he becomes silent and appears to start crying, wiping a tear from the side of his face.... [H]e reaches toward the camera and shuts it off."

Their final tape is less than two minutes long. Eric, behind the camera, tells Dylan to "say it now."

"Hey, Mom. Gotta go," Dylan says to the camera. "It's about half an hour before our little judgment day. I just wanted to apologize to you guys for any crap this might instigate as far as (inaudible) or something. Just know that I'm going to a better place than here. I didn't like life too much and I know I'll be happier wherever the fuck I go. So I'm gone."

My parents have only seen the tape once. The police refuse to release it to the public, citing fears of copycats. However, it is clear simply from the tapes' excerpts that much could be learned from them about Eric and Dylan's true motives.

What angers me about the videotapes is that none of Eric and Dylan's friends have ever been allowed to see them. Think about it. You have three hours of video, recorded by two teenagers full of rage about our school. They reference song lyrics. They reference things at Columbine. Who is going to understand those references? Other kids.

But at this time—three years after the shootings—the only people who have seen the videotapes are detectives, reporters, and the families of the victims. These adults won't catch the references that Eric and Dylan's friends and classmates will.

I believe the tapes can help us understand what happened and should be released to the public. However, if the judge isn't willing to do that, the police should at least put together a group of high school students, as well as some of Eric and Dylan's friends, and have them watch the tapes. It amazes me that investigators have not done this, because who knows what clues are flying right over their heads?

The police don't think people need to know anything more about Eric and Dylan's motives. But I want a chance to learn from those tapes for myself.

It remains to be seen whether any of us will have that chance.

Shortly after the *TIME* article about the videotapes was released, a small item appeared in the media. Undersheriff John Dunaway formally announced that I had nothing to do with the attack on Columbine.

"There is no evidence suggesting Brooks Brown was in any way involved in these murders," Dunaway said on December 21.

Nonetheless, the damage had already been done, and my family would never forget. And before long, we would be given the chance to fight back.

18

TO THIS DAY, THE HARRIS AND KLEBOLD FAMILIES HAVE REFUSED TO grant any media interviews. They have also never met with the families of the victims. However, the week before the one-year anniversary of the Columbine attack, both families issued statements to the media.

The Harris family wrote:

We continue to be profoundly saddened by the suffering of so many that has resulted from the acts of our son. We loved our son dearly, and search our souls daily for some glimmer of a reason why he would have done such a horrible thing. What he did was unforgivable and beyond our capacity to understand. The passage of time has yet to lessen the pain.

We are thankful to those who have kept us in their thoughts and prayers.

—Wayne and Kathy Harris

The Klebolds offered their own statement of sympathy:

Nearly a year has passed since tragedy changed the Columbine community forever. A day that began innocently ended catastroph-

ically. The healing process has moved slowly as we all attempt to cope, not only with our own despair, but also with the distractions and intrusions that result from world attention.

There are no words that convey how sorry we are for the pain that has been brought upon the community as a result of our son's actions. The pain of others compounds our own as we struggle to live a life without the son we cherished. In the reality of the Columbine tragedy and its aftermath, we look with the rest of the world to understand how such a thing could happen.

We are convinced that the only way to truly honor all of the victims of this and other related tragedies is to move clearly and methodically toward an understanding of why they occur, so that we may try to prevent this kind of madness from ever happening again. It is our intention to work for this end, believing that answers are probably within reach, but that they will not be simple. We envision a time when circumstances will allow us to join with those who share our desire to understand. In the meantime, we again express our profound condolences to those whose lives have been so tragically altered. We look forward to a day when all of our pain is replaced by peace and acceptance.

Finally, we wish to thank those who have sent their kind thoughts, prayers and expressions of support to our family. We are constantly surprised and heartened by the gestures of understanding and compassion that have been extended to us. The support has been both humbling and inspiring, and we are truly indebted to those who have offered it.

—The Klebold family

I haven't seen the Harrises since the day Eric threw a piece of ice into my windshield. I know nothing about what their life has been like since April 20. However, my family did keep in touch with the Klebolds.

I visited Dylan's parents at their home one day, about a year after the murders. Mrs. Klebold made strawberry shortcake, and we sat down in their living room and caught up. We avoided the subject of Columbine for a long time; we talked about their house, where I was going with my life, how my parents were doing. They were trying so hard to be normal. But the conversation eventually turned toward Dylan.

It was awkward; I didn't know what to say. I could talk to them about what was happening with the police, or what it was like at the school, or what I was doing. But it was hard to talk about Dylan.

When I left, it was for the last time. I've never been back.

My mother has attempted to maintain her friendship with Mrs. Klebold as best she can. However, it's hard for them to talk without the subject of Dylan coming up, and that causes Mrs. Klebold a lot of pain. The Klebolds go day-to-day, because with Columbine, you never know if something new is going to be in the paper tomorrow—something that will bring it all back again.

Reminders of Columbine never stopped coming. In fact, new tragedies continued to compound our community's suffering.

Six months after the murders, the mother of one of Columbine's injured students committed suicide. Carla Hochhalter walked into a Littleton pawnshop, asked to see a gun, and agreed to purchase it. As the clerk turned his back to gather the necessary paperwork, Hochhalter loaded the gun and shot herself.

Her daughter, Anne-Marie Hochhalter, had been wounded in Columbine's parking lot. Carla Hochhalter had already been suffering from depression for several years; her illness worsened after her daughter was injured, and she was hospitalized several months before her death. Some consider her to be one more of Eric and Dylan's victims.

In February, two Columbine students were gunned down at a Subway restaurant just a few blocks south of the school. Nicholas Kunselman was an employee at Subway and had just closed the store for the night. His girlfriend, Stephanie Hart, was there with him. Sometime between 10 p.m. and 1 a.m., both were shot and killed. No money was taken from the store, and there was no clear motive. To this day, the police have made no arrests in the case.

Only a few weeks after the one-year anniversary, Columbine basketball player Greg Barnes committed suicide. Barnes was in the choir room when Eric and Dylan went on their rampage. I never knew Greg, but from what people have told me, the memories of that day were too much for him to deal with.

Of course, seeing things like that happen worsened the pain everyone was feeling. A year after the murders, I was still struggling with what had happened that day. No matter how much I analyzed it, I still didn't understand why my friends had done what they'd done. I still had nightmares about the shootings. I still asked myself if there was something I could have done.

There was no peace to be found. No easy answers. No closure.

On April 20, 2000, Colorado Governor Bill Owens called for a moment of silence to remember the shootings at Columbine. "Today is about the angels who are watching over us, helping us to heal and helping us to remember," he said outside the state Capitol in downtown Denver.

At a private tribute to students and teachers, Principal Frank DeAngelis read the words of President Clinton to an audience of over a thousand in the Columbine gymnasium.

"What happened in Littleton pierced the soul of America," Clinton wrote, according to the Rocky Mountain News. *"Though a year has passed, time has not dimmed our memory or softened our grief at the loss of so many whose lives were cut off in the promise of youth."*

As they had done a year before, media trucks gathered in Clement Park to record these events. Many were preparing stories of healing and closure.

Away from it all, Brooks stood alone, smoking a cigarette and remembering.

Contrary to what some in the community were saying, the one-year anniversary had nothing to do with closure—at least, not for those closest to the tragedy. That week, the families of fifteen people killed or wounded at Columbine filed suit against the Jefferson County Sheriff's Department.

The Sanders family sued because Mr. Sanders had been left to die in the school, even though the police knew for hours where he was. The police didn't reach Sanders until 2:42 p.m. From there, they made the students who were caring for him evacuate. Yet, even after they had reached the room, it took over half an hour for paramedics to be brought in. By that point, it had been nearly four hours since Sanders had been shot. He bled to death.

Other lawsuits used the Web pages my family had turned over to argue that the police could have stopped the massacre from happening, but didn't.

Sheriff Stone called the lawsuits "ridiculous."

"We didn't do anything wrong," he told the Rocky Mountain News. "We have people who did some pretty heroic things that are now getting kicked in the face for rescuing people, for saving people's lives. Because of greed."

Heroic? How? Who had they actually saved? The police stood outside and did nothing during the entire massacre. Not one officer attempted to engage Eric and Dylan after entering the school. Mr. Sanders was alive for three hours before officers even reached him. Lives could have been saved if the police had gone in, but they didn't. Stone was trying to portray his police force as a noble organization that had done everything it could. However, the events of the next month would show just what kind of police force we were really dealing with.

A month after the first anniversary, the Jefferson County Sheriff's Office released its official report on the Columbine killings. The bulk of the report was a timeline showing the events of April 20.

This was how the police described my last conversation with Eric:

"Harris speaks to one student briefly outside the west entrance of the school. According to the student, Harris tells him to leave the school because he likes him. Shortly thereafter, the same student is seen by witnesses walking south on Pierce Street away from the area. This student is the only person Harris and Klebold direct away from the school grounds moments before the killing begins."

This description was incorrect. I never spoke to Eric outside the west entrance. I spoke to him in the parking lot near the east entrance—on the opposite side of the school. On paper, it seems like a small mistake. Yet Eric and Dylan reportedly started their shooting at the west entrance. Saying that I met Eric there implies that I saw guns, ran away without warning anyone—and ran to the other side of the school in order to be moving south on Pierce later.

Was it a mistake? If so, I can't help questioning the accuracy of the rest of the police report. On the other hand, perhaps it was intentional. After all, putting me at the west entrance certainly makes me look suspicious to anyone who reads the report.

The police made brief mention of Eric's Web pages in the report, but played them down. "The information was reviewed by Sheriff's investigators," the report reads. "However, Harris's Web site could not be accessed nor could reports of pipe bomb detonations be substantiated. Because of Brown's request to remain anonymous, Klebold and Harris were not contacted. Further investigation was initiated but no additional information was developed."

This was incorrect, too. My family did not request to remain anonymous. We asked that the Harris family not be given our name, but my father offered to sign a police report; he was told that would not be necessary. Also, my parents were told in their meeting with Detective Hicks that there were reports of bomb activity in our area, so "reports of pipe bomb detonations" *were* substantiated. And if the police were having problems accessing Eric's Web site, they could have called us back and asked for help. They never did.

The Sheriff's Report was supposed to answer all of the public's questions about Columbine. Instead, the more I read, the angrier I became.

Sheriff Stone and the Jefferson County Police Department continued to infuriate survivors of Columbine as the summer progressed. In June, Sheriff Stone was asked to testify before the Columbine Review Commission, an investigative panel assembled by Governor Owens. Stone originally said he would, but the day before his scheduled testimony in June, he changed his mind.

Stone told reporters he had "no choice" because of the lawsuits his department was facing from the victims' families. He had been advised by attorneys not to testify. He stood by that decision, even as Governor Owens himself urged Stone to change his mind.

Stone also refused to hand over Danny Rohrbough's clothing to his parents, even though other parents had received their children's possessions long ago. The police told Brian Rohrbough that Danny's shirt was a biohazard. Then they claimed that they wouldn't hand it over because the case was still open. This seemed odd to observers; after all, by now the police had publicly stated that Eric and Dylan had been the only ones involved in the killings. However, as long as the case wasn't closed, the police weren't obligated to hand over evidence.

Frustrations such as these motivated the Browns—with the blessing of several of the victims' families—to launch a recall effort against Sheriff Stone. By June 9, 2000, their recall petition was approved by the Jefferson County Clerk's Office. They would have sixty days to gather at least 42,000 signatures from registered voters.

The petition listed four reasons for Stone's recall:

1. Because Sheriff Stone has lost our confidence and trust.
2. Because he has put his political career ahead of the interests of the citizens of Jefferson County.
3. Because he has mismanaged the Columbine investigation.
4. Because he has mismanaged the sheriff's department during his term in office.

Randy Brown pointed to the TIME debacle, the suspicion cast on Brooks, and the behavior of police at Columbine on April 20 as examples of inexcusable behavior by Stone.

"Why aren't people mad?" Randy Brown told the Rocky Mountain News. *"Don't they get it? They let children die. Innocent, defenseless children were murdered while they waited outside, and that was a command decision by Sheriff Stone."*

However, the recall effort proved too daunting a task for the Browns and the handful of volunteers who joined them. While the Browns gathered a substantial number of signatures, they couldn't reach their goal by the time the sixty-day period was up.

Even though their effort had fallen short, the Browns still wanted to make a statement. Fearing retribution by Stone against those who had signed the petition—including officers in his own department—the Browns chose not to turn those names in. Instead, they chose to leave just two names on the final petition. Their own.

My family's battle with Sheriff Stone taught me an important lesson about politics. When my parents were circulating that petition, people would say to them, "If he weren't doing his job, he would be fired." People have to understand that when it comes to elected officials, we, the public, are their bosses. We hire them through our votes. We are also the only ones who can fire them.

Too many people ignore politics in their lives, refusing to vote or get involved in the process. Yet even the smallest and most unimportant elected official will affect them.

For elected officials, character has to matter, because they are setting an example for the rest of us. The President of the United States sets that standard. Yet who was President when Columbine happened? It was Bill Clinton, who was embroiled in the Monica Lewinsky scandal, getting oral sex from an intern in the Oval Office and then lying under oath about it. If that's the example we get from the highest elected official in the land,

and he suffers no real penalty, then why would anyone bat an eye if Sheriff Stone lies to parents about what happened to their children at Columbine?

Young people see adults lying and getting away with it on a regular basis. That's the example being set for us.

That's why people in our country must pay attention to what's happening in the world around them. I don't see how anyone who reads up on Columbine would come away believing the police did nothing wrong. Yet for many, when it comes to difficult issues, it's easier to just look the other way.

19

the truth comes out

UNHAPPY WITH THE LACK OF INFORMATION IN THE SHERIFF'S REPORT, families of Columbine victims continued to push for the release of all information related to the investigation. In November of 2000, that wish was granted.

Judge Brooke Jackson ordered the release of over 11,000 pages of investigative files on November 21. Jackson outlined specific exceptions to that instruction: crime scene photos, autopsy reports, and material seized from Eric and Dylan's homes were not to be released. Neither were details about the bombs, or Eric's "hit list" of people he wanted dead. However, all other material was to be handed over.

The Jeffco Sheriff's Office charged $602 for each copy of the materials, claiming that the charge would cover printing costs. My parents obtained one of the sets and immediately pored over it, hunting for new information.

There were some surprises among the pages. We learned that while the Klebold family had given an extensive interview to police, there was no report of an interview with the Harrises. The police said that they hadn't gleaned enough information from their sole interview to write up a report.

In addition, we read that the Harrises had resisted the arrival of police at their home on April 20, 1999. At first, they barred officers from their home. Then they tried to stop them from going down into the basement, where Eric's bedroom was.

"Mr. and Mrs. Harris were afraid of retaliation from the parents [whose] children were killed at [the] high school," read part of the report.

There were reports of more warning signs from Eric and Dylan before the attack. According to the report, Dylan was fired from his job at Blackjack Pizza for bringing a pipe bomb to work. Yet store owner Bob Kirgis told police that Eric brought a pipe bomb to work in April of 1997 and talked about detonating it; Kirgis took no action against him.

The report contained a short story written by Dylan in our creative writing class. I had never seen it before. In the story, Dylan described a man dressed in a black overcoat who "looked ready for a small war with whoever came across his way." The man confronted a group of "college-preps," one of whom he described as a "power-hungry prick." The man then drew weapons on the group and began shooting. "The shining of the streetlights caused a visible reflection off the droplets of blood as they flew away from the skull," Dylan wrote.

The final portion gave a glimpse of what was going on in Dylan's mind:

> The man then pulled out of the duffel bag what looked to be some type of electronic device. I saw him tweak the dials, and press a button. I heard a faint, yet powerful explosion, I would have to guess about six miles away. Then another one occurred closer. After recalling the night many times, I finally understood that these were diversions, to attract the cops.
>
> The last prep was bawling and trying to crawl away. The man walked up behind him. I remember the sound of the impact well. The man came down with his left hand right on the prep's head. The metal piece did its work, as I saw his hand buried about 2 inches into the guy's skull. The man pulled his arm out and

stood, unmoving, for about a minute. The town was utterly still, except for the faint wail of police sirens.

The man picked up the bag and his clips, and proceeded to walk back the way he came. I was still as he came my way again. He stopped, and gave me a look I will never forget. If I could face an emotion of god, it would have looked like this man. I not only saw in his face, but also felt eminating [sic] from him power, complacence, closure and godliness. The man smiled, and in that instant, through no endeavor of my own, I understood his actions.

The thousands of new pages of evidence would prove to be an invaluable resource in researching what happened at Columbine. However, there was little new information on my family, or Eric's Web pages, in that massive report. Despite the 11,000 pages of material, we suspected that the police were still withholding information from the public.

On the morning of Columbine's two-year anniversary, I was driving through Clement Park with a friend on our way to the memorial ceremony. My friend noticed a camera operator unloading equipment from the back of his truck.

"Hey, look—media guy," my friend joked. "How many points do I get if I aim for him?"

I shook my head. "I have no problem with the media," I said. "Where would Martin Luther King have been if there weren't any cameras?"

I know it's popular in many circles to bash the media; people in Littleton do it all the time. I won't join them. I've met a countless number of reporters in the three years since Columbine; not only did most of them prove to be great people, but we would never have uncovered the information we did without them.

It was the media that showed us what Eric and Dylan said on their basement videotapes. It was the media that kept constant pressure on the police to release more information. And when the media reported Sheriff Stone's comments about my "involvement" in the murders early on, they also gave my family plenty of chances to respond on the same day. They treated us with fairness.

In fact, I owe a debt of gratitude to the producers of CBS's *60 Minutes II*. Thanks to their work, it was finally proved—after two years of doubt—that my family had been telling the truth from the beginning.

Producers from *60 Minutes II* arrived in Littleton sometime between January and February of 2001. They were aware of the many new developments in the Columbine case, and wanted to dedicate a full hour to reporting on it—an unusual move, since they usually have three or four different stories per show.

Much of their report was dedicated to the police response to Columbine, and whether more could have been done. In interviews with Ed Bradley, I recounted the story of Eric's Web pages yet again.

While *60 Minutes II* was in town, my parents received a letter from Jefferson County District Attorney Dave Thomas. We had asked for an internal investigation of Columbine back in October, and he was writing to tell us that the investigation would not happen; one reason he listed was that he had seen an affidavit for a search warrant of the Harris home in 1998, and it was not enough reason for a new investigation.

We were taken aback. No search warrant had been released among the 11,000 pages of police reports. If one existed, it would prove that everything my parents had been saying for the past two years was true. The police had insisted that there had been no follow-up investigation, that the Web site couldn't be accessed, and that my parents had never met with Detective Hicks or with the bomb squad. If a search warrant was out there, it was imperative that we get hold of it to prove them wrong.

My parents faxed a copy of the letter to *60 Minutes II*. From there, CBS took the ball and ran with it. The show's attorney went to Jeffco with the letter in hand and demanded that the search warrant be released. With their help, we uncovered the truth.

The release of the search warrant was major news in Denver. For the Browns, it marked vindication after two years of being told they were lying.

The affidavit was prepared by the Jefferson County Sheriff's Office in March of 1998. According to the affidavit, a pipe bomb that had been found in a field one month before matched Eric Harris's description of his homemade bombs on his Web site.

Bomb squad member Mike Guerra wrote in the affidavit that "the size (of the bombs) is consistent with the devices labeled by Harris as 'Atlanta' and 'Phobus.' " Yet the proposed search warrant had never been presented to a judge.

"I'm happy to learn more of the truth," Brian Rohrbough told CNN on April 10. "They had denied this application existed. Columbine should never have happened. It begs the question, 'Why did you deceive everyone?' "

A month later, Sheriff Stone would claim that "there was no attempt to hide documents" showing that investigators wanted to search Eric Harris's home in 1998. "I thought it was fairly well known," he said in a television interview. "We weren't trying to hide anything.... Nobody asked for it."

Stone's assertion was false. Judge Brooke Jackson had ordered the sheriff's department to release all of its Columbine files, except for those the judge specifically wanted withheld. By not releasing the affidavit, police had directly disobeyed the judge's order.

"People criticize the media for being negative," Randy Brown says today. "I'll tell you, the Sheriff's Department was lying to us for two years, and none of this would have gotten out if it weren't for the media. Without them, we would be nowhere."

It meant everything to my family to finally have proof that we'd been telling the truth. But at the same time, it was hard to be happy when we saw that search warrant. Had the warrant been approved by a judge, I believe everything would have been different. The police would have found the pipe bombs. They would have found Eric's journals, and the violent writings on his computer. He would have been stopped.

Instead, that chance slipped through the cracks.

20

final hope

OVER A YEAR AFTER JUDGE BROOKE JACKSON ORDERED THE RELEASE of all Columbine material, the new revelations kept coming.

In March of 2002, crime-scene photos from the Columbine murders were leaked to the media. The Rocky Mountain News *published a detailed account of the photos, but spared the public from the sight of them; however, the paper also cautioned that the photos were circulating throughout Denver. The* Denver Post *warned that it was only a matter of time before the photos were picked up by a tabloid or posted on the Internet.*

Randy Brown condemned Stone for the mistake, saying that if his office couldn't even keep crime scene photos under wraps, he should resign. Parents of the victims were horrified; Tom Mauser told the Rocky Mountain News, *"If it was their child that was murdered, would they want that picture shown to other people? It's beyond me."*

It wasn't the first such leak. In November 2001, the journals of Eric Harris were also leaked to the media. Those journals contained detailed plans by Harris to attack Columbine High School, as well as an entry that described in detail what Harris wanted to do to Brooks. Harris had been plotting to break into the Brown home on the morning of the attack, kill Brooks and his family, and burn down their house before moving on to Columbine and continuing the slaughter there.

Had the search warrant drafted by the police been served, these writings probably would have been found as well.

In late 2001, a witness came forward to say that a member of the SWAT team at Columbine feared he had "accidentally shot a student" during the attack. According to Brian Rohrbough, that student was his son Daniel. Bullet shells from police were found all around Daniel's body, and investigators recovered only one of the three bullets that killed him. Furthermore, police officer Jim Taylor told Brian Rohrbough that he had seen Daniel killed while running from Eric and Dylan—which didn't explain how Daniel was shot from the front, at the angle of someone below him.

Daniel's parents tape-recorded this conversation. When the police issued a statement from Taylor saying he had never told Brian he'd seen Daniel shot, Brian produced the tape. Taylor was placed on leave the next day.

Despite these new revelations, in November 2001 U.S. District Judge Lewis Babcock threw out all of the Columbine families' lawsuits except that of Angela Sanders. The judge described the slow police response to dying teacher Dave Sanders as "shocking to the conscience of this federal court."

However, he wrote in response to the other suits that "holding police officers liable in hindsight for every injurious consequence of their actions would paralyze the functions of law enforcement."

Under pressure, Sheriff Stone asked investigators from the nearby El Paso County Sheriff's Office to conduct their own investigation of Rohrbough's death. However, the investigation would be conducted behind closed doors, with no involvement from the families—and no promise of new information.

With the support of Colorado Governor Bill Owens, the victims' families requested that a grand jury be convened to investigate Columbine.

That request was denied. The families were told by U.S. Attorney John Suthers that even if there was evidence linking a police officer with Daniel Rohrbough's death, Suthers still wouldn't see reason to call for such an investigation.

The families had one option left. They pressed for a legislative investigation of the Columbine massacre at the state level. They received backing from State Representative Don Lee, who proposed a bill creating a committee that would have full subpoena powers.

This would be the first-ever investigation to have that ability; the Columbine Review Commission had been unable to force Sheriff Stone or other responding officers to testify. The committee would also be able to subpoena records that were not available to the general public.

On March 8, 2002, survivors and their families went to the state capital for a hearing to determine whether such a panel would be created. The House Civil Justice and Judiciary Committee conducted the hearing.

The lawsuits had been thrown out. Open-records requests had failed. This was the families' last chance to learn the truth about what had happened at Columbine.

Brooks and his parents made plans to speak before the committee that day. It was the first time Brooks would appear in public alongside the parents of the kids he had been accused of plotting against.

I arrived at the hearing a few minutes late. I'd given Richard Castaldo a ride there, and we'd been held up by the downtown Denver traffic. By the time we arrived and got Richard's wheelchair unloaded and assembled, Representative Lee had already given his opening statement.

However, I was there in time to see the Jefferson County Sheriff's Office put on a show as it defended its actions.

Investigator Kate Battan and Jeffco's attorney, Bill Tuthill, sat before the committee as their assistants wheeled boxes of evidence files into the room. I heard one of the victims' parents compare it to the scene in *Miracle on 34th Street* where all of the letters get brought into the court-room and dumped on the judge's desk, overflowing onto the floor.

Tuthill described how open his department had been with the public. "The Jefferson County Sheriff's Department, over the course of the last few years, has produced a phenomenal, unheralded amount of material in unprecedented volumes during this particular investigation," he said. "They are available not only to the news media, but to the families of the victims and to the public at large.

"The truth is, contrary to what you may read in the papers or hear from some constituents, a wealth of information concerning what hap-pened at Columbine High School has already been produced," Tuthill continued. "There is no need to go through this legislative inquiry in order to obtain additional information."

The floor was opened to comments from the public. The first to speak were those opposed; one of them, Rachel Erbert, was a former classmate of mine.

"I think the answers that many people are looking for, to give closure, are not going to be found out in this lifetime," she said. "For me person-ally, I can't get closure with this in the newspaper every single day. And I think it's going to increase the hurt."

Another local resident went on to criticize my father and Brian Rohrbough at length, referring to their efforts as "bulldog persistence." The speaker, who claimed that his wife, a reporter, had been "trauma-tized" by a story she did on Columbine, said there would be no purpose served by any further investigation.

"Every time this comes up on the front page ... it's re-traumatizing people who were involved," he said. "Some of these people are family members, some of them are students who were in the school, some of them are people in the sheriff's department.... Is it worth going through this process again for what little we're going to learn? I don't think it is."

I looked over at Richard, watching the proceedings intently from his wheelchair. We spoke briefly, and with only a few minutes to spare, I began penciling in some changes to the speech I was about to give. Then they called my name.

I came forward and sat down before the nine-member committee. Behind me were the Rohrboughs and the Petrones, the Velasquezes and the Kechters, the Flemings, Lauren Townsend's mother, my parents, my friends ... and on the other side, there was Kate Battan, and the representatives of the Jefferson County Sheriff's Office.

I cleared my throat and began.

I'm Brooks Brown, and I'm here representing myself. I would like to apologize, because Richard Castaldo won't be testifying. He really didn't have too much to say. He's been rather sad lately. But he and I talk a lot about Columbine. He and I have kind of grown into a friendship.

I've seen Richie change. I saw him before Columbine; he was a real outgoing kid. He's changed a lot since it happened. Yet I sat back there and I asked him, after I heard all those people testify, whether he feels "traumatized."

You see, Richie's paralyzed. You can't miss him; he's back there in the wheelchair, because he got shot in the spine. But he hears about Columbine, and it doesn't re-traumatize him.

In my case, my friends did this. And I was called "murderer" for months afterward. John Stone maligned my name many times. So did other people, saying I was a possible suspect. And my parents, as you saw up here—Randy and Judy Brown—they are maligned all the time.

It doesn't re-traumatize them. It doesn't re-traumatize me. It makes me sad, but it doesn't re-traumatize me.

There are a lot of kids who remember what that school was, and they remember what Eric and Dylan and people like me went through—the outcasts. They look at it in a different way than most of the other people do. They won't be here testifying today, because they're scared that what happened to me may happen to them.

They say we've learned lessons from Columbine; I would like to state that while we may have—and while we may have become more strict about certain things—there were still things before Columbine that were illegal, and Eric and Dylan got away with them.

It was still illegal in Jeffco, before Columbine, to create pipe bombs. My parents and I reported a Web page where Eric laid out detailed plans about these pipe bombs. His names for them. What he wanted to do with them. And on there, he wished that he could kill me.

We reported it, but somehow Eric got away with it. They would probably jump on it now, if they had a second chance; they probably wouldn't want all of this egg on their face. But it still happened back then. They did prepare a search warrant; thanks to 60 Minutes II, *we did find that. But we don't know why it was stopped. Why all of that happened is a question that I personally want answered.*

I heard the first speaker say this, and it's something that was rather upsetting. They said that Eric and Dylan wished they would get this kind of fame.

Eric and Dylan are dead. They lost. They died that day. And if you're religious, they are in hell. Having a bad time. They did not win.

What we are to do is to come away from this and learn things from it. We are to learn what happened beforehand. What led up to it. That includes the school. That includes bullying. I know when I spoke with Representative Lee before, he mentioned that he wanted to talk to some of the students without any subpoenas, so as not to re-traumatize them. I thought that was great. I could get him a number of students who could do it. They want to talk about how that school was. They want people to know. They just don't want to be called a murderer, or "hateful." It's not that fun.

Richie will never get closure. I will never get closure. This will be a mark on my future forever. Kids died. They were shot. Other kids ran over their bodies. Other kids had to lie there and watch their friends die. This isn't something you get closure for. This is something that you learn to deal with.

There is hate of the government. It's starting with teens, and you see it all over the place. There is a distrust. We watched on April 20 as cops stood outside while kids died inside. While a teacher died inside. We see this, and we see them give out medals.

There is something wrong in this police department. And that is why I hope, Representative Lee, that you push this through. Because there is a lot to be learned. Thank you.

The chairman opened the floor to questions. Representative Shawn Mitchell pointed out that my concerns about Columbine were more expansive than what the proposed committee would cover. He asked if I still felt the committee would be worthwhile if it didn't address those questions.

"I completely understand that," I replied. "But my feelings are that once you get into one part of it—as I'm sure anyone who has gone into the pages in-depth has—you will find that one thing leads to another, which leads to another, which leads to another. And it kind of snowballs, and you slowly see how this huge thing built up. While it may be extremely expansive, it's all there. And you'll see it."

There were no further questions. My testimony concluded, I sat down as my father took his place before the committee.

"Today, you were all lied to by the Jefferson County attorney," he said. "And I can prove that."

My father described his long battle to extract information from the Jefferson County Sheriff's Office. He talked about filing requests for police maps through the Freedom of Information Act, and being told that he was being given every map available. Later, in a conference room, he saw maps that he had not been given, and photographed them. Now my father presented those photographs to the committee as proof that the police had lied.

My father went on to say:

> I believe that Jefferson County has withheld a great deal of information. To document that further, we have a photograph of John Kiekbusch with 300 notebooks, instead of the pitifully small amount shown here. We also have another attorney for another lawsuit, who says that Jefferson County has told him that there are 54 "banker boxes" of evidence files. You see before you approximately five.
>
> Distrust of the government is the main key here. I'm forty-nine years old. I'm a taxpayer. I no longer trust Jefferson County

in any way. I have been lied to by so many people there that there are very few people there I would trust with any result. And I believe it's possible that if I feel that way, then many other people feel that way. That possibly, Columbine is going to have the end result of losing public confidence in the government in general.

Until somebody does something—and gentlemen, that's your job. It will happen right here, or it won't happen.

My mother spoke before the committee next. She described the ordeal our family had been through ever since we found Eric's Web pages, and noted that nowhere in the released Columbine files is there any record of her meeting with Detective Hicks. She argued that a legislative committee would have the subpoena power necessary to get to the bottom of what happened:

My questions are: What happened to my report? What happened to every report? What do I need to do differently as a citizen? Should I still call the police? Should I still assume they are doing their job? I want to know what I can do differently; to this day, I do not know.

When people call me—when parents call me because they know I was in this situation, and they ask me what should they do—I don't know what to tell them. Would I trust the police? Absolutely not. I would not trust the police. I don't know what to do, and that's wrong.

Before all of this happened, I put all of my faith—I put my son's life—in the hands of the police. Now, my son is here today, and I am very fortunate that my sons are here. But there are other people behind me whose kids are NOT here, and this is wrong.

And if you don't find this important enough to find out what hap-
pened in this police department, so that we can know and be
assured these corrections can be made ... If they will not
address what happened to our stuff—how can we know that the
police are following up on these things? How do we know that
changes are being made?

Committee member Alice Madden tried to sympathize with my mother, telling her she worried that the families "wouldn't walk away with the truth."

"I think the worst thing that could happen is to go through this and not give you the answers that you want," Madden said. "I worry about a political body in an election year, doing this ..."

"This may be our last hope," my mother quickly replied. "I think it would be worthwhile if you could get at least some of the things out. A lot of important changes could be made. We really need to get into the deeper issues, and find out the truth. We need to find out what happens when a citizen goes to the police, and what they should expect....

"We're telling kids, 'Report it.' For what? What are they going to do? We don't have answers, and it's been almost three years. In truth, I don't know where to go next."

The first of the Columbine victims' parents to speak was Dawn Anna, mother of Lauren Townsend.

"The worst action you could take today is inaction," she told them. "Ladies and gentlemen, if you don't try, we may never know the truth about what happened. You represent me. Us. People of Colorado. Does that also include children?"

Mrs. Anna brought up questions about how her daughter had died in the library, and asked why the police had made no move to stop it:

> I have serious questions about the timeline where my daughter is concerned, as well as other children who were killed....
>
> I have questions when there is an open line recording the murders one by one, and the injuries occurring in the library one by one, and we know the location of the two murderers in the library. We know what they're doing: they are injuring and murdering children.
>
> They have a specific location... and then, as the two murderers leave the library, the children who are able to get up and run out. They run to a door that leads to the exterior, to the outside. They come through that door and into the waiting arms of uniformed officers. And many of them are telling those officers two very important things: that there are children injured and possibly dead in that room, and that the two murderers [have] left, and that is why they were able to escape.
>
> Yet those same policemen do not go through the doors those children just safely exited. In fact, the library is one of the last places [the police reached]. I don't know why. I have heard that they thought the door was booby-trapped. Yet all these children who survived that attack just ran through that door.
>
> I have heard that they thought bodies were booby-trapped. Danny's body, Rachel's body, were moved. The children coming out of that library who said the murderers were gone said nothing about booby-trapped bodies. Yet it takes four hours to get into that library.
>
> These are serious, serious questions that I have. And your body, with subpoena power, can bring forth some of those

policemen who are wanting to testify and provide that kind of information. They've never been able to provide it.

Mrs. Anna noted that many of the families are in therapy, and that the only way to truly find closure is to understand what happened. She argued:

> *We have to face what happened that day, and in the days fol-lowing, so that then we can progress down the road to recovery.*
>
> *How can we do that with the truth still hidden, rewritten, destroyed, and covered up?*
>
> *You don't have to know exactly what to do with the informa-tion you uncover during this investigation. You simply need to begin the process. A process—the only one so far—with sub-poena power, to allow those who have been waiting to be deposed and come forward and testify, and let the truth out. The courts, the judges, the lawyers, the therapists, the educators can take whatever information you find to the next level, so that all of those processes can begin to finally heal our community, and heal our nation.*
>
> *Please don't let the costs of this investigation be your moti-vating factor in deciding whether you do this investigation. In fact, they should not be a factor at all. The cost of NOT doing this investigation will be incalculable. The lack of faith and trust in our legislators will be a high toll. The cost of the next massacre, wherever that may occur, will be immeasurable. I do not want to be the one who tells people like those of Santee, California, that an investigation could have led to the prevention of the murders at that school, but the cost was too high.*

Am I reaching too far with this reasoning? You know I am not. There will be more tragedy in our schools. Why? Because we have no answers here. Our past will be, because it has already become, our future, if we don't change. If we don't act.

Brian Rohrbough followed Mrs. Anna. He told the committee, "All I want is the truth," and detailed the discrepancies over his son's death. "When we asked them questions about it, they absolutely refused to answer," he said of the police. "We asked for additional meetings; they refused. Our only answers came from going to court in an open-records case, and by filing a lawsuit. And we should not have had to do that."

Mr. Rohrbough also brought up the search warrant, adding that it might have kept the entire Columbine incident from ever happening. He wanted to know why it had never been served.

"One or two people who are dishonest can discredit an entire agency," he said. "And I would like you to put faith back in government. To show the people that the police really are accountable. I think this committee can do that."

Kyle Velasquez's father, Al, also spoke to the committee about his son. The police had told him that Kyle was killed instantly in the library, and that he had no idea what was happening. Yet Mr. Velasquez learned later that his son was found curled up underneath a table in the library, hiding from Eric and Dylan.

"Can you imagine what happens to us when we find out the truth?" he said. "It's like it happened again.

"I honestly believe that you are our last hope," he continued. "I'm asking you, please. In the memory of our kids, help us."

❖

The committee took a brief recess while the rest of us stood outside, not knowing what would happen. By now, we had heard three hours of testimony. Every aspect of the case, from Eric and Dylan's motives to the immediate police response to Sheriff Stone's behavior in the years afterward, had been laid out on the table. It was in the committee's hands.

Discussion of the proposal was very brief. Lee defended it one last time, arguing that, while Columbine had been investigated before, a legislative committee would grant the subpoena power necessary to extract new information.

"There have been a lot of issues raised today," he said. "And I'm not saying that I think this committee is going to get into those specifics. But through the documents that we obtain, and the testimony of people who thus far have either been less inclined to testify because of litigation, or have not been totally open, it gives us an opportunity."

The committee members responded with nothing but doubts.

"I guess my fear is that this task force is going to create false hopes that we will be able to deal with all these issues," said Representative Betty Boyd.

"You've had no answers in the past," added Representative Jim Snook. "You have a lot of questions. You haven't been satisfied with the answers you got, or else you got no answers. I'm of the judgment that the answers you're going to get, if this committee is successful, will be vague answers."

The chairman put the resolution to vote as the room fell silent.

"Bacon."

"No."

"Boyd."

"No."

"Jahn."

"No."

"Johnson."

"No."

"Madden."

"No."

"Snook."

"No."

"Stengel."

Stengel took a moment. "This is the hardest vote I ever gave. No."

The recorder turned to Representative Lee and called his name.

"Yes," Lee said, the defeat in his voice apparent.

"Mr. Chairman."

"Yes."

Even as he offered the only other favorable vote, Chairman Shawn Mitchell knew it was already over. "That motion fails, 7 to 2," he said. "There is a motion to postpone indefinitely the resolution, forwarded by Representative Madden and seconded by Representative Bacon. Please call the roll."

Again, the vote was 7 to 2.

At the back of the room, my father stood up and looked down the row of the House Civil Justice and Judiciary Committee.

"Shame on you," he said quietly.

We had no idea that the deck had been stacked against us from the start.

The next day, the *Rocky Mountain News* ran a story entitled "Jeffco Pressured Lawmakers." According to writer Kevin Vaughn, officials from Jefferson County had been actively lobbying against the investigation behind closed doors, even inviting the committee members to their offices to discuss the bill. The officials kept this information secret from Representative Lee, who was sponsoring the bill.

We had no idea about this at the time. We had no idea that the police had already influenced the committee members before we even walked in the door. We believed that our words were going to make a difference.

Now the hope we had been filled with when we walked into that room was gone. We exited in defeat, realizing that at last we had come to the end of the road. There would be no answers. The police had won.

I gave my mother a hug, then went outside to smoke a cigarette with my friends, stunned by the injustice of it all. I helped Richard into the front seat, then loaded up his wheelchair and started the car. We drove quietly through the streets of downtown Denver, headed for home.

"It makes you wonder what the system is there for," Richard said after a moment.

I looked over at him. I recognized the look of hopelessness in his face.

21

hollow victory

IN THE SPRING OF 2002, THERE WERE OVER A DOZEN CANDIDATES lining up to take on John Stone for the role of Jefferson County Sheriff. Many of the victims' families braced for what was sure to be an ugly, drawn-out campaign that fall. However, Stone saved them the trouble.

On April 5, Stone announced that he wouldn't be seeking re-election. He told the media that while his office had been a "dream job," the Columbine massacre had turned it into a "nightmare" and a "living hell."

"We did the best we could under impossible circumstances and have been punished for it ever since," he told the *Denver Post*.

"You've got a tar baby that no matter who touched it, they are not going to walk away from it," he told the *Rocky Mountain News*. "I still think we did everything we could do [at Columbine] under impossible circumstances and by the rules—as the rules were at that time."

My parents issued their own joint statement in response to Stone's announcement.

"His arrogance has been unbelievable to us," they said. "It is about time he admitted to himself that the people of Jeffco don't want a man who is so deceitful and lacking in character as John P. Stone."

On April 11, The El Paso County Sheriff's Office completed its four-month probe into Daniel Rohrbough's death. The Jefferson County Sheriff's Office had asked El Paso to do its own independent review of how Daniel had been shot, to clear up questions brought forth by Daniel's father, Brian. Not only had Brian produced evidence arguing that Dylan Klebold could not have shot Daniel, but he had further suggested that a police officer might have been the shooter instead. Among the evidence Brian Rohrbough pointed to was the trajectory of the bullets that hit Daniel, the fact that police shells were found all around his body, and that two of the three bullets that hit him were never found.

For over a week, the public wasn't told what El Paso had found. Jefferson County District Attorney Dave Thomas said he wouldn't be releasing its contents until after the three-year anniversary of the shootings on April 20, "out of respect for the Columbine community."

In response, Brian Rohrbough called for the report's immediate release, as did the families of other Columbine victims. Thomas relented, and on April 17—three days before the anniversary—the public learned what El Paso had found.

El Paso cleared the police of having shot Daniel Rohrbough, but they also found that things had happened differently than Jefferson County had claimed in its original report two years before. Ballistics determined that Eric Harris, not Dylan Klebold, had fired the deadly shots.

"The murder of Daniel Rohrbough at Columbine High School on April 20, 1999, was undeniably caused by Eric Harris beyond any reasonable doubt," read the report summary.

The week before the three-year anniversary of Columbine, my parents told me we were going to a screening of a new A&E documentary, *Columbine: Understanding Why*. The hour-long show, part of A&E's

Investigative Reports series, centered on a group of forensic scientists who had spent months conducting a "psychiatric autopsy" of Eric and Dylan, in an attempt to determine why they'd done what they'd done. The team was made up of a psychiatrist, a violence prevention expert, a former FBI profiler, and a doctoral candidate.

The documentary had attracted attention because it had been specifically requested by the district attorney back in 1999. Because of that, we were curious about what this team had been granted access to, and what they might have uncovered.

My family watched the show alongside the families of Daniel Rohrbough, Kyle Velasquez, and Kelly Fleming. It was the first time I had seen Mrs. Fleming since that day at her house the summer after the shootings. It never stops feeling awkward to be in a room with the parents of a Columbine victim, no matter how many times I see them. The guilt I feel for having been friends with their children's killers never really leaves me.

However, that night we were united in our disappointment over the investigative team's effort. After a long recapping of the shooting, complete with drum-heavy atmospheric music, the investigators talked about the lengthy research they were going to do.

"As they conduct their psychiatric autopsy of the Columbine High School killers, Eric Harris and Dylan Klebold, the threat assessment group needs to talk to as many people as possible who knew the boys throughout different stages and in different situations in their lives."

That's funny, I thought. I don't ever remember these people calling me.

Not only that, but the documentary never mentioned the Web pages my family turned in. There were flaws throughout the piece, but this was a glaring omission. That and the pro-police slant of the documentary were what really bothered me.

The victims' families mentioned to the *Rocky Mountain News* reporters that it seemed like the district attorney had been far more help-ful to outside investigators than he had been to any of them. I sat there contemplating that, and realizing that what we'd just seen was going to be aired to the nation in just a few more days.

If people don't already know what happened here, this is the version they will believe, I thought. *People will believe that the police did every-thing they could. People will believe that there were no obvious warning signs. People will believe that this couldn't have been prevented.*

I thought back to a quote from Mark Twain.

"Truth is stranger than fiction," he said. "Because fiction has to make sense."

The truth was that the victims' families had reached the end of the road.

After the defeat of the proposed legislative commission to investigate Columbine, Representative Don Lee of Littleton made a second attempt. This time, instead of a sweeping probe of the Columbine incident, Lee narrowed the proposed investigation to three questions:

- *What can be learned from the law enforcement response on April 20, 1999, in preparation for another attack?*
- *What can be learned from the response to the complaint filed with the Jefferson County Sheriff's Office alleging that gunman Eric Harris was making death threats over the Internet?*
- *What can be learned in regard to destructive behavior exhibited in the school environment by the perpetrators in the time leading up to the attack?*

At first, the newly refined proposal met with success. The bill passed through the House State, Veterans and Military Affairs Committee on an 8–1 vote, and then on through the full House on a 39–24 vote. But the bill was defeated by the Senate Judiciary Committee with a 4–3 vote. Even with a narrowed focus, lawmakers did not feel the need to investigate Columbine any further.

"We fought a good fight," Lee told the Denver Post on May 7. "I don't regret putting all of my efforts into doing the right thing."

In a study released on May 14, 2002 by the National School Board Association, seventy-seven percent of 837 school board members polled across the country considered school violence to be a "moderate" or "mild" concern. Only one in nine educators called it a "major concern." The week before the survey came out, a student in Ehrfurt, Germany, opened fire at his high school, killing seventeen before turning the gun on himself.

On April 18, 2002—two days before the three-year anniversary of the Columbine shootings—two Columbine High School students were suspended after they left a hit list written on a wooden pillar in Clement Park. The list named eleven students and two staff members. The students face criminal charges.

While many were turning their backs on the events of Columbine, one investigative team remained. A records review task force, made up of both law enforcement officials and members of the community, was going through the remaining Columbine evidence that had not yet been released by the courts.

On April 17, in a moment that shocked many observers, the panel named its newest member: Randy Brown. Colorado Attorney General Ken Salazar appointed him in the belief that Brown would ask the right questions.

"This gives the committee credibility in the eyes of the victims' families," Brian Rohrbough told Kevin Simpson of the Denver Post. *"Very few people have studied the volumes of records like he has—and nobody who's not involved in litigation or a member of the media. Putting Randy on lets us know that the committee will have to consider everything."*

Randy Brown said later that Salazar's decision was a positive step forward.

"I really couldn't believe it when they asked me," he said. *"My wife and I had met with Salazar only a few days beforehand, and he didn't give any indication that he was thinking about doing this. But I think he wants to get to the truth of what happened, so it was very encouraging."*

As soon as he was asked to join, Brown started talking to people to find out what evidence they still believed hadn't been released. He already had a list of fifty-nine items that he had presented at a previous meeting.

"What they've promised is that we will get to see everything the police have," he said. *"And then we'll offer our opinions on which of those files should be made public."*

Brown made it clear that he supported releasing Eric and Dylan's basement tapes, to help the public understand why they did what they did. To allay fears that the tapes could lead to copycat violence, Brown said the photos of Eric and Dylan lying dead in the library should be released as well.

"If there are people who think that Eric and Dylan were heroes, those photos will take away that 'hero' status right away," he said. *"No matter how messed up someone is, I don't see how they could think that Eric and Dylan did anything glorious after seeing how they ended up."*

However, Brown was interested in more than just releasing what the public already knew existed. Soon after his appointment, Brown showed the rest of the committee a page from the recently released El Paso report. The page looked like a duplicate of evidence provided by Jefferson

County in its public report, but it had a different index number from the one in the files released to the public.

Brown pointed to that discrepancy as evidence that Jefferson County had been withholding information, and wanted to ask investigator Kate Battan about it.

Battan didn't attend the meeting. Her spokeswoman said she had fallen ill.

Finding out that my father would be on the task force was incredible news. It was like one small victory after years of defeat.

As of this writing, the task force's work is still not finished. I don't know whether Eric and Dylan's videotapes will ever be released to the public or not, or whether new evidence will be uncovered that none of us have ever seen before. Like everything else in Jefferson County's handling of the Columbine case, it's a mystery.

However, one new piece of evidence concerning my family did see the light of day. By court order, the Jefferson County police were forced to release copies of all search warrants from the day of the shooting, including the warrants for both the Harris and Klebold residences, and lists of all items seized from those locations.

In the search warrant for Dylan Klebold's home, among the items investigators said they wanted to find were "any information on Eric Harris's Web page, Web site or in his e-mail file, namely http://members.aol.com/rebdomine.pissed.htm."

On April 21, 1999, another search warrant noted:

Your affiant discovered a report made to the Jefferson County Sheriff's Office on March 18, 1998, 98-5504, by Randy

Brown. Randy Brown stated that Eric Harris was making death threats toward his son, Brooks Brown. Randy Brown provided ten pages of material copied from Eric Harris's Web page to Deputy Mark Miller. One of the printouts reads, "Wie gehts. Well all you people out there can just kiss my ass and die. From now on I don't give a fuck what almost any of you mutha fuckas have to say, unless I respect you which is highly unlikely, but for those of you who know me and know that I respect you may peace be with you and don't be in my line of fire. For the rest of you, you all better fucking hide in your houses because im comin [sic] for EVERYONE soon, and I WILL be armed to the fuckin teeth and I WILL shoot to kill and I will fucking KILL EVERYTHING!" (Jefferson County Search Warrant, Investigator Cheryl Zimmerman, 4/21/99)

I wasn't expecting this at all.

As I read it, the anger built up within me. A year ago, *60 Minutes II* had uncovered the draft for a search warrant in 1998 that never was served; that was hard enough to learn about. But now, here was written proof that within a day of the shooting, they'd used the information my family had provided to search the homes of Eric and Dylan. They'd had all the variations of a Web address that they'd claimed they weren't able to access. They'd had specific quotes from the Web pages, including the death threats. They'd had everything. And while they were using this information to obtain search warrants, they'd called my family liars for claiming that we'd warned them. They'd pointed fingers at me as a possible suspect. They'd turned everyone against me.

And they knew. The whole time.

This was vindication, even more than the search warrant a year ago had been. But it didn't make me feel any better. I didn't want to see this information handed down now, when it wouldn't do any good anymore.

I wanted it used in 1998. I wanted Eric Harris caught.

I wanted Columbine never to have happened.

No matter what we learn about the police behavior that day, or what they did to me, or to my family—no matter how much vindication I might find—it will always be a hollow victory. Search warrants won't bring Danny Rohrbough back to life, or Rachel, or Kyle, or any of them. They won't give back Richard's ability to walk. They won't save Eric and Dylan from becoming what they became.

It's important to know the truth. It's important to keep going, and not to lose hope in the face of the police.

But it won't ever give us back what we lost that day.

22

little brother

EACH DAY ANOTHER MIND IN OUR WORLD IS CRIPPLED. ANOTHER child gives up. Another kid kills his friends, or himself. Many people say that this happens because the child loses hope.

People ask all the time why Eric Harris and Dylan Klebold did what they did on April 20, 1999. I believe it was hopelessness. They saw no real future for themselves, and no acceptance from those around them. They became self-hating. Then they started to hate those around them. Then they became angry, and then they became violent. Finally, in one insane, twisted moment, they believed they had power over a world that had kept them down.

Eric and Dylan came at Columbine from different places. Eric was mentally imbalanced. He had clear bipolar tendencies and was being treated with medication. He had a fascination with death, with firearms, and with rising above his tormenters, and his mental instability fueled that.

Dylan was angry with society, with the hand he had been dealt, and with a world where he couldn't go a day without being spat at, mocked, or told he wasn't good enough. He was made to believe that his dreams could never happen, and that the world would never get better.

This is the hopelessness that many kids in high school share.

What was unusual about Eric and Dylan was the way they withdrew from everyone else and fed each other's delusions. They kept their beliefs to themselves, figuring the rest of the world would never understand them. They developed God complexes. What shreds of ethics they may have had left were destroyed as they retreated more and more into their own world.

Eric was probably the one who formulated the plan for attacking Columbine. Yet he and Dylan had become so close that it was easy for him to convince his friend. "We don't have to take this shit lying down," I imagine them thinking. "These fucks don't deserve to live. They aren't even on our level. We understand what the world is about. They don't. Just think what kind of an impact we could have—what kind of a statement we could make—if we did this."

To the rest of us, it sounds insane. Perhaps if Eric had said this when he and Dylan first met, Dylan would have thought it insane as well. But with the formation of that bond that only the closest of friends can know, Dylan came to look up to Eric. He trusted in him. He wasn't getting the answers he wanted anywhere else.

I knew Dylan long enough to know that he didn't start out as a monster. He became one. That's what makes his fate so scary.

The next Dylan could be your son. Your neighbor. Your best friend. Not some faceless, anonymous killer who comes out of the dark and snatches your loved ones. A regular person who faces the cruelty of the real world just like the rest of us—and in whom something erodes away over time.

It's too late to stop Eric and Dylan. But maybe if we realize what we're doing to one another and take action now, we can save the kids who would otherwise go down the same path.

Not all kids become hopeless at an early age like Eric and Dylan did. Some hold on to their ideals, and fight for change. I respect them so much, because, as I learned, the political machine can prove a formidable challenge.

In the summer of 2001, I got a call from David Winkler of SAFE Colorado. SAFE (Sane Alternatives to the Firearms Epidemic) Colorado is a group of teenage activists based in Denver. They often make trips to Washington, D.C. to lobby senators and congressmen; Winkler told me they were planning such a trip for late July. Their purpose was to fight for a change in gun show legislation, one that would require all sellers to run background checks on customers.

I agreed to go along. This would be my first chance to visit the nation's capital as a lobbyist, meet with politicians, and get an up-close look at the political machine.

We were hit with disappointment once we arrived. One of our own state representatives, Republican Scott McIniss of Grand Junction, refused to so much as meet with us. His spokesman argued that because McIniss had met with members of the group two years ago—right after the Columbine shootings—and because SAFE Colorado had a different stance on guns than he did, he didn't care to speak with us on this trip.

"We feel their points are the same and our points are the same, so there's really not much more to discuss," spokesman Blain Rethmeier told the *Rocky Mountain News.*

On the way to Washington, I'd talked with a lot of the SAFE Colorado kids. They were smart, idealistic kids who believed they could make a difference. Now they were being told that their own congressman wouldn't give them the time of day.

We did get to meet with other members of Congress. It was educational, to say the least. I had come for an up-close look at what the system was really like, and that's exactly what I got.

People talk all the time about how Washington is corrupt. It's not exactly a revelation. However, it's a different experience to be in the halls of Congress, talking with a senator, when her aide informs her that one of her allies has suddenly switched his vote. She looks down and says under her breath, "Well, I wonder what he got."

At one point I was in the room with two congressmen, and I overheard one of them talking with his aide. They were preparing a photo with members of the SAFE Colorado contingent. The congressman asked, "Did you make sure you have a mixed bag of races?"

I tried to do some lobbying with a freshman representative. He wasn't there when I came to his office, but his aides talked to me. They were extremely honest about their stance on gun control. "Here's how it is," one of them said. "We're brand new in this office; we still don't understand how Congress works. All I know is that what helped us get here is our gun stance, and we can't change that or else the National Rifle Association will take our funding away. So what else can we do?"

I appreciated that honesty, even if the message was pretty upsetting. Many other members of Congress wouldn't even talk to us, or else they dodged our questions.

After our first day of lobbying, I sat around talking with other kids from SAFE Colorado. They were so frustrated. Most of them were younger than me, and they were so full of ideals. They really cared. They wanted to bring about change.

The experience of seeing Washington in action had brought many of them down. They were realizing that this trip wasn't going to affect anything; the system was far too massive and corrupt for them to change. All that went through my mind was that this was the moment when their hope was being broken, like so many others before them.

That thought affected the hell out of me. I had seen enough hopelessness. It was time to prove that we could get something done.

I sat down with David Winkler and Ben Gelt, two other guys from the program. They felt the same way I did. After brainstorming, we came up with an idea for a new project. Using their camera, the three of us wanted to find the top six senators and congressmen who were opposed to gun legislation and get interviews with them on tape. We could then put together a film about our experiences once we got home.

In particular, we thought back to Representative Scott McIniss, who had snubbed our group the day before. We were going to make him talk to us, one way or another.

The next day, Ben and I went to McIniss's office with Ben's video camera. We said we were making a movie about gun control, and that we wanted to get McIniss's comments on tape. They told us to sign in.

We knew McIniss was aware that SAFE Colorado was in town, and an article with my name had already appeared in the news; if I signed in as Brooks Brown, there was no way in hell that he'd talk to us. So I gave a fake name, and said nothing of our being involved with SAFE Colorado.

Unfortunately, someone in McIniss's office recognized me, because they tipped off the Congressman. He in turn called Mike Sprengelmeyer, a reporter for the *Rocky Mountain News*'s Washington bureau. He told Sprengelmeyer that we were trying to perpetuate fraud.

The next morning, we were called into an emergency meeting with the heads of SAFE Colorado. John Head, the organization's attorney, told us we had disgraced them. He said what we had done was unprofessional, and that it wouldn't be condoned by SAFE. They told us to leave immediately. The three of us were given plane tickets, put in a cab, and sent home.

We were angry. Maybe we shouldn't have used a fake name, we thought, but we were honest with McIniss about why we were there. The questions we planned to ask were worthwhile. All we wanted was to finally get McIniss to talk to us, since he'd turned the group down before. Two other representatives we'd contacted were willing to talk to us on camera; we had a legitimate project.

Most of all, we were trying to change something for the other kids in the group. We wanted them to get something out of this trip after all.

David tried to explain our actions to the *Rocky Mountain News*. "The sad thing here is, the point was lost that we were simply trying to get the Congressman to explain his position," he said. "Instead, they're seeing this as an excuse to throw out some students who are obviously committed."

I agreed completely. We had all learned that as long as the jerks are in power, regular people have no influence. I had already learned that lesson from Sheriff Stone; now I had learned it in the halls of Congress. We'd learned it from the people who wouldn't talk to us. We'd learned it from the congressmen who had showed us firsthand how difficult it was to go against the system. We'd seen that money controls everything in Washington. We'd seen that for the individual who wants to bring about change, the political road is one roadblock after another.

I was frustrated. But I wasn't going to give up.

That same summer, I got my first chance to make an impact on the system. That chance came courtesy of filmmaker Michael Moore.

An in-your-face investigator, Moore developed his reputation in the 1980s with his landmark documentary *Roger & Me*. The movie was about Moore's attempts to meet with Roger Smith, the CEO of General Motors, in the wake of a major factory closing in Michigan. After that, he worked on investigative-reporting shows like *TV Nation* and *The Awful Truth*, while continuing to make documentary films. He has also written two books: *Downsize This!* and *Stupid White Men, and Other Sorry Excuses for the State of the Nation*.

What I liked about Moore was his style. He doesn't play games with people or try to ingratiate himself. He simply tells people what's going on, in a tone with a humorous edge to it.

I first met Moore when he was filming a documentary about guns and youth violence, called *Bowling for Columbine*. He wanted to know if I would participate. I was more than happy to.

Several months later, I heard from him again. He called me up to say he was making a visit to Kmart's headquarters in Michigan to ask them to stop selling handgun ammunition in their stores. Eric and Dylan had purchased their ammunition at Kmart, so it made sense that Moore asked me if I wanted to come along.

I wasn't the only one; Moore invited two other Columbine students, Richard Castaldo and Mark Taylor, as well. The three of us flew in from Colorado in early June, 2001.

The next morning, we were picked up at the hotel and went straight over to Kmart's headquarters, where we met up with Moore and his film crew. We wanted to meet with the CEO of the company. Instead, Kmart sent down their head of public relations, a guy from buying, and a guy from risk management.

With Moore's cameras rolling, the three of us met with them and told our story. I talked about growing up with Dylan, and my last conversation with Eric. Richard and Mark talked about their injuries; Mark had been shot on the hill outside the school, not far from Richard. Both of them described the years of grueling physical therapy they'd undergone as a result of the shootings.

Both Richard and Mark still have bullets from Kmart lodged in them. Moore reminded the executives of this more than once, referring to my friends as "the Blue Light Special." Richard and Mark even lifted up their shirts to show their scars to the executives.

Since we were dealing with a corporation, we didn't know what effect, if any, our words would have. Yet the Kmart executives didn't seem to resent our presence. None of them was a typical "corporate stooge." They listened to us. One even had tears in his eyes as we told our stories.

At the end of our meeting, they told us they weren't going to commit to any decision—basically the response we had expected. We left feeling like we were off to a good start but still had a lot of work ahead of us.

The next morning, Moore called a press conference outside Kmart's headquarters. We figured that we were in for several days of keeping up the pressure on the corporation. After all, if you've ever seen Moore's other work, you know that executives usually ask him to leave, push him out the door, and refuse to speak with him again—and by now, Moore knew how to fight back.

This time, he didn't have to. Less than an hour after we arrived, Kmart announced that they were going to pull all handgun ammunition off their store shelves by the end of September.

We had succeeded.

Kmart claimed that they had been planning this move for months, and that our presentation hadn't had anything to do with the decision; whether that's actually true is subject to debate. But that first day, we showed them that we weren't going to give up. From what we could tell, it had paid off.

For the first time in a long while, I felt positive about the world. First, I had gained so much respect for Kmart. Here was a corporation that went against the norm. Instead of chasing us out, or hitting us with bureaucracy, they'd invited us in, listened to our concerns, and reacted. That impressed the hell out of me. In addition, we had just removed a way for teenage gunmen to acquire ammunition. I don't support gun control, but I do support enforcing the laws we have—and it would be a lot easier for a kid to buy bullets from some teenage clerk at Kmart than from the owner of a gun shop. If closing this avenue discouraged just one potential shooter from imitating Columbine, I considered it a victory.

A victory for the individual, achieved without help from the government or the police. A victory realized not by a committee, but by a filmmaker and three teenagers.

A sign that maybe there was still hope after all.

Working with Michael Moore was an inspiration. He saw problems in the world and took action against them as an individual, in his own way. I wanted to make a contribution as well. Perhaps I could use what I had experienced to make a difference in some way. I knew there were other kids out there who felt lost and alone, just like Eric and Dylan did. I wanted to find them. I wanted to reach out to them before it was too late.

I just had to figure out how.

One of my first inspirations came from music. At a KottonMouth Kings concert in Denver, I encountered a band I'd never heard of before, called Corporate Avenger. Many of their lyrics centered on the injustice of the government and the theft of land from Native American people. In other words, this band was about more than just making music. These guys were interested in making people think. As luck would have it, I ran into a few members of the band after the show, and we got into a long conversation.

We spoke at length about the idea that music had caused Columbine; they felt it was ludicrous. They made it clear that they were artists expressing ideas, but that they weren't advocating violence in any way. In fact, they were committed to opposing violence and fear as a means of imposing thoughts and ideas. They believed in nonviolent expression of thought, and protecting freedom of speech.

I mentioned that I wanted to start some kind of group for society's thinkers—people like us, who wanted to change things through logic and reason rather than force or violence. They told me they would love to be involved in something like that. We talked about using the Internet some-how for that purpose.

I left that night with a new focus. I would try to reach out to the other individuals of the world. The thinkers. The people who wanted to make a difference in society. It was just a matter of deciding how to implement it.

Soon I had an idea.

By now, I had accumulated experience designing Web sites. It occurred to me that I could create a place on the Internet for those who thought outside the norm to share their thoughts with one another. I wanted to give people a chance to see: "Hey, there are other people who are having problems like mine. They think the world sucks just like I do. But they're advocating that we do something to change things, through logic and nonviolent resistance. Hey—maybe there's something to this."

I named the Web site Little Brother, a reference to George Orwell's *1984*. In that book, a government known as "Big Brother" controlled its citizens' every move. I compared that to our government, and chose "Little Brother" to describe a group of concerned citizens, considerably smaller than Big Brother, who are watching the government the same way that the government is watching us.

For the Web address, I chose www.atlasisshrugging.com (now www.atlasisshrugging.org). The first essay I posted on the site presented thought as the enemy of evil:

> *The arguments evil uses to win are not logic, but feelings. Not hope, but despair. Not reality, but some sort of super-reality that none of us can hope to achieve. But we, the good, use three simple things to prove our points: Reality, truth, and life. We*

*simply want the truth, and we only deal in the truth. We have the
chance to take back the world that is rightfully ours.*
   Don't let them win.

The original Web site was little more than a message board for people interested in philosophy. A person could post his or her thoughts
about the world, and I or someone else on the board would respond.
Then we would get into a discussion. Sometimes we approached difficult topics, like whether or not the government should retaliate against
the Taliban for the September 11, 2001 attacks. It didn't matter what
your personal beliefs might be—you signed on to this site to see a mil-
lion perspectives.

   I didn't promote the site at first. I mentioned it to a few of my friends,
and asked them to refer anyone who they thought would be interested.
When forty different people signed in within a week, I thought, "Shit.
Maybe there's something to this."

   For a few months, I left the site alone, to see how it would grow.

   In the meantime, I corresponded with a guy who called himself
Middle Brother—a brilliant philosopher and a genius at Web page design.
He liked the idea behind Little Brother and offered his services to help
revamp it. Together, we created new forums and posted philosophical
essays on the main page.

   A wide variety of posters began arriving: a teenager nicknamed
"DeadBoy," who ranted against the injustice of high school but also
preached nonviolence. "Miz," a free-thinking girl in California. A guy from
Iowa who nicknamed himself after Hank Reardon, a key character from
Ayn Rand's *Atlas Shrugged.* The list kept growing. People wanted to talk.
They had a thirst for conversation, for thinking and debating.

   We put up a questionnaire for new participants to fill in. I wanted to
see where people were coming from and adjust our site's direction

accordingly. After all, I don't pretend to have all the answers to society's problems. I simply wanted my site to be a gathering place for those who were dissatisfied with the way things are. By talking through our problems together—and realizing we weren't alone in the world—we were starting something. Who knew where we might go from there?

Ever since it happened, Columbine has maintained a large presence on the Internet. Multiple discussion boards, Web sites, and tribute pages still circulate through cyberspace, and people trade information all the time.

I have mixed feelings about this. Many of the sites have good intentions. There are memorials to the victims, posted so that people will never forget what happened. Other sites are investigative sites, which support the contention that the police are still holding back evidence. Those sites are good to see. They show me that, three years later, people still care. They're still asking questions.

There are some other Columbine-related sites that are a little more ... well ... disturbing. I've read conspiracy theories from people who believe Eric and Dylan were part of a government mind-control plot, that they were "brainwashed" to attack Columbine. After all, these conspiracy buffs argue, the government wants guns out of the people's hands, and what better way to do that than stage a "school shooting" so that people get angry and demand gun control? I swear, I'm not making this up.

Then there are the obsessive types. Girls will write about how they are "in love" with Eric and Dylan. Some have gone so far as to write about wanting to "dig them up and make love to their headless corpses." Others pretend to be students from Columbine. I entered a chat room discussion with a guy who swore up and down that his name was Brooks Brown, and that he'd graduated from Columbine High School in 1999. I was just like, "Um, I'm pretty sure you're not, dude ..."

I don't pay much attention to these people. But the kids who intrigue me are the ones who write about how they idolize Eric and Dylan, or call them heroes. They write that Eric and Dylan made a "brave" choice by attacking their high school, and that it sent a message to all the jocks and bullies of the world.

These people have a horribly skewed outlook on life—but at the same time, I recognize what's happening to them. They may not have started out any different from you or me. But they've become so frustrated with the world that in their anger they look upon two mass murderers and actually see reason there.

Some of the posters on Little Brother asked me if I was worried that sooner or later those types of messages would show up on my board. The truth is, I hope that people who feel that way will use the Web site. After all, why would people post messages about how much they admire Eric and Dylan? Because they're going through the same kind of shit Eric and Dylan did, and they feel so alone that they think only Eric and Dylan would have understood. Yet by reading just a few of the posts on our board, they can see that there are people who are having the same kinds of problems they are, but are staying in touch with reality.

Maybe it will help them to reevaluate. Maybe it will help them realize that a lot of people are screwed over by the system, but that doesn't give them a reason to become like Eric and Dylan.

If even one of them starts to think twice about idolizing Eric and Dylan, or imitating them, then my site has served its purpose. The answer to feeling alienated isn't to do what Eric and Dylan did. It isn't to give up. It isn't to kill.

It's to use your mind, and make things better.

23

where do we go?

I'M STANDING IN CLEMENT PARK, AT A MEMORIAL SERVICE FOR Columbine's victims. It's April 20, 2002.

I can't believe it's been three years since it happened.

In one more month, the Columbine High School Class of 2002 will graduate. These are the last kids who were there when Eric and Dylan took their revenge. Starting next year, there will be all new students at Columbine—students who have no firsthand memories of hiding in their classrooms, or running away as bullets flew overhead. They will have no memory of seeing friends turn into mass murderers. They will have a clean slate.

The Columbine library is gone, demolished nearly two years ago. It's been replaced by an atrium. The place where Rachel Scott was killed is gone, covered up by an entryway that links to the new library. The patch of asphalt where Danny Rohrbough was killed is no longer there; that entire concrete stairway was pulled up and remodeled.

If you don't know what happened there, Columbine High School looks like any other school in America.

Some students tell the newspapers now that there is no bullying at Columbine. Others say the bullying is so bad that they're glad graduation is finally coming.

In today's newspaper, a teacher said that when she hears the claims about bullying at Columbine, "I think sometimes we feel like the rape victim who's told her skirt was too short and she shouldn't walk down the street at night."

Attempts are already being made to rewrite history. Also in this morning's paper, a Columbine teacher told the reporter, "[Harris and Klebold] scared me more than any other kids in the building. They bullied more kids than they were bullied."

Now, walking with my friends toward the memorial service, I see that same teacher moving in the opposite direction. I glare at her as I walk past. She doesn't return my gaze.

Some choose to deal with Columbine through ignorance. But the memories of that day can never be covered up for long. Nor can the repercussions.

Even though the cloud of Columbine will hang over us for the rest of our lives, all of us are trying to move on as best we can.

My brother graduated from Columbine High School last year. He's thrown himself into composing music, recording demo CDs for friends and spending entire nights hunched over his synthesizer. Music has always been his passion, and I imagine it always will be.

Trevor and I are still close friends. When memories of Columbine really start to weigh me down, he's the best confidant I have. He was there with me the whole way. Most of the time, though, we just have a beer or play a good video game, and concentrate on happier times.

From time to time, I still see guys like Nick Baumgart, Zach Heckler, and Chris Morris around town. Sometimes we nod. Sometimes we talk. But there's distance there now. I imagine it will always be that way.

I moved out of my parents' house a couple of years ago; now I live with friends in an apartment across town. Like any family, my parents and I still have our arguments and our rough times. But we've grown much closer since Columbine happened. In fact, I got my father to go with me to Detroit and attend a Twiztid concert. Imagine my dad, surrounded by juggalos with their faces painted and chains hanging off their clothing! It was a good time.

These past three years have been difficult. Even today, I'm still not over what happened. I go through major mood swings and depressions, something I never had to deal with before April 20. I do different things to cope with it. Sometimes I go online, sometimes I play a video game, some nights I wind up drinking. I'm doing much better today than I was a few years ago, but things can be hard sometimes.

Lots of things trigger painful memories—not just when I drive past the school or hear Columbine mentioned in a news report. There are little things, too. Maybe I'll buy a new multi-player computer game, and as I start to play, suddenly I'll wonder what Dylan would have thought of it. And then I'll get angry with him and Eric again, for having done something so stupid and cruel. We had so many good times, and those memories are forever tainted now. I hate them for having betrayed me like this. For having betrayed all of us.

But things are getting better. I've realized something important over the past three years: In spite of the hell that I lived through, I am still alive. I'm one of the lucky ones.

As we stand there at the anniversary ceremony, the time reaches 11:19. Principal DeAngelis is reading the names of the thirteen who died. As he reads each one, a balloon is released into the air. Kyle Velasquez's parents are standing a few feet to the left of me. When I hear his name, I see the balloon leave their hands and float away, joining the others already disappearing into the distance.

Walking away from the ceremony, I glance over at the sidewalk, about a hundred yards away, where I stood three years ago. Where I saw Eric pull in. For the past two years, I marked this anniversary by standing in that spot.

I don't feel compelled to do that this time.

One reason is because of what happened last year. That day, I was standing there, just as I had the year before, smoking a cigarette and remembering. Then the police pulled up and demanded my name. The public had been banned from entering Columbine on the anniversary, and apparently the sidewalk out front was considered part of school property. I tried to explain that I was a former student, and was mourning my friends, but they didn't care. They ordered me to leave.

Back then, I was so shocked by their actions that I complied. But I'd had a year since then to fume over the memory. I knew that if I went over there today and they tried to make me leave again, my response would probably get me into a lot of trouble. Since harassment from the police wasn't how I wanted to spend this day, I decided against going to "my spot."

Besides, in some ways it was a healthy decision. Standing there with a cigarette, remembering Eric's car pull in, helped me for the first couple of years after the tragedy. But that moment doesn't define me. Who I am from this day forward is what defines me.

I don't know where my Web site will go. It is simply my personal attempt to make a difference. Yet that's my point. If each of us quits complaining about the world—and instead takes action in his or her unique way—who knows what could be accomplished? I don't want to mark the deaths at Columbine with a "moment of silence" anymore. I want to mark it with moments of action. For me, those moments include helping with Michael Moore's project, or working on my Web site, or telling my story.

I want people to learn from what happened here, and I want them to keep asking questions.

When it comes to Columbine, some solutions are more obvious than others. We have to crack down on all forms of bullying. Obviously, this means the kids on the playground who beat up the outcasts, or the high schoolers who mock and harass the kids wearing black and keeping to themselves. But we also have to look at teachers. Teachers who only like the "good kids" and turn their backs on the rest are causing untold pain and anger in those forgotten students. If students are given up on early, then they learn to hate the system and can no longer be rescued by it.

We have to reevaluate what we as a society are doing to our children. They, and not our careers or our personal lives, must be our priority. When people choose to become parents, they must make those children their primary focus—not just say it, but live it. Our kids need that kind of guidance in today's world.

Humanity has not changed in several millennia, even if our technology has. Because of technology, we can survive twice as long as we could a few hundred years ago—yet most of us accomplish only half as much. We can find out any fact we want through the Internet—and many of us want porn and hate.

As the writer Jhonen Vasquez said, whether in a loincloth or business suit, we're the same.

Why do people wonder where Eric and Dylan came from?

I guess they ask because they never look at themselves.

We as a society allowed Eric and Dylan's creation. If we sit back and wait for society to fix itself, it will never happen. We will only see more of the same.

But if we as individuals choose to do something, then it's the first step toward change.

I saw my best friend from grade school become a mass murderer. I saw my report to the police get swept right under the rug. I was asked by my own school never to come back. I was called a killer on the street. I saw the families of murdered children lied to for three years, then saw our lawmakers tell them there was no reason to investigate it.

I saw all of this, and I haven't given up.

Neither should the rest of the world. If there's one lesson to be learned from Columbine, it's that we can't let things remain the way they are. We can't succumb to feeling powerless against the world.

Learn from the injustice of Columbine. Look for where parallels are happening elsewhere. I guarantee, you won't have to look far. Then fight to change it. Don't wait for everyone else. Don't let the world happen around you. Don't stay powerless.

Don't give up hope.

24

IN THE FOUR YEARS SINCE WE TURNED IN THE FINAL DRAFT OF *NO EASY Answers,* the Columbine story has continued to unfold.

Rather than a full disclosure of evidence, the Jefferson County Sheriff's Office has kept releasing new revelations piece by piece—right up to the time of this writing, in fact, when we got our first glimpse at notebooks and journals that were seized from the Harris and Klebold homes. Each piece helps to form a more complete picture of what happened and why, but the new information also leads to new questions.

Shortly before we began our initial publicity tour for *No Easy Answers* in the fall of 2002, the public got its first look at Eric Harris's Juvenile Diversion report. Eric and Dylan had been ordered to participate in Diversion, a police intervention program, after their arrest in the 1998 van incident. On his Diversion evaluation, Eric marked for police that he was "suicidal" and "homicidal." The two of us discussed this surprising information on CNN, pointing out yet another red flag that had been missed.

As could be expected, memories of Columbine continued to fade in the public eye, save for the occasional pop culture reference. By the summer of 2003, many of the lawsuits by families of the victims had been settled. The Klebolds and the Harrises gave depositions to police, finally discussing at length what they had seen and heard in the months leading up to the massacre. However, those depositions were sealed as a condition of the settlement. They have yet to be seen by the public.

In the fall of 2003, police released the "Rampart Range" video of Eric and Dylan conducting target practice in the woods, getting a feel for the weapons they would later use in their assault. More tapes would be released the following spring, including the infamous "Hitman For Hire" tape and footage of Eric and Dylan hanging out with fellow students in Columbine hallways and the cafeteria. The basement tapes, though, still remained under wraps.

We attended a public viewing of Columbine evidence at the Jefferson County Fairgrounds in February of 2004. There are no words for what we saw. Destroyed chairs, bullet fragments and shattered computer screens sat on display shelves or inside plastic evidence bags. The harsh reality of these objects, which had once seemed to exist only in photos or police reports, was jarring. The murder weapons themselves, still covered with fingerprint dust and residue, were grouped together in a glass case at the far corner of one room. The unexploded propane tanks were there. So was the bloody clothing. So was the famous "1 Bleeding To Death" window sign. So were the pipe bombs.

We said little, simply moving from display to display as we attempted to take it all in. We had come there because we felt that we needed to, but once in that room—surrounded by researchers, current and former Columbine students, police and softly weeping members of the public—the true chaos of it overwhelmed us. It was important to see it once. Neither of us wanted to see it again.

At first, mourners and media heavily attended the anniversaries of Columbine. By the four-year mark, though, April 20 had become such a non-issue that the two of us were able to pay our respects right there on school grounds at 11:19 a.m. It was a massive contrast from the crowds and police barricades of previous years.

However, for the five-year anniversary in 2004, people came back. A large crowd gathered in Clement Park to listen to local officials and family members, who shared their thoughts as the sun set on an evening memorial service. They pledged not to forget what had happened here.

Once *No Easy Answers* was released, we made that our mission as well. The two of us spoke to high school assemblies, conferences and educators around the country, from Chicago and Cedar Rapids to San Diego and Las Vegas.

In speaking with students, we'd ask the same question: "How many of you remember where you were when you first heard about Columbine?" Virtually every hand would go up. For better or worse, the shootings had been a defining moment for the youths of our generation. Even students who had been in grade school when Columbine happened had a strong interest in it.

Students would ask us, "Could something like Columbine happen here?" Each time, we would answer without hesitation: Yes, of course it could. Not because their schools were rife with problems or their kids were especially violent. It was because something like Columbine could happen anywhere, and no one should turn a blind eye.

A lot of students said they recognized what Eric and Dylan were angry about. No one we talked to would condone what the killers did. But they did acknowledge that they knew kids who had expressed similar frustrations with the system, or shown hatred for themselves and their school, or been misunderstood by teachers and classmates. These students would hang around long after the regular sessions were over, asking questions or sharing their experiences. Several teachers told us that youths in their classes who normally kept quiet or wouldn't participate in discussions paid close attention to us, and were quick to engage us in conversation afterward. It meant a lot to hear that.

Eric and Dylan have continued to remain cult heroes to some. Shortly after a programmer used home RPG-maker software to build a video game called *Super Columbine Massacre RPG*, a visit to the discussion forum on his website at www.columbinegame.com revealed just how many kids—kids whose ages were still in the single digits when Columbine happened—idolize the two killers.

These kids constantly say things like, "Eric and Dylan struck a blow for bullied kids everywhere." They conveniently leave out the fact that Eric and Dylan didn't kill bullies, but instead shot innocent kids like Rachel Scott. We mentioned kids like these in the first edition of this book, and four years later, their numbers seem to hold strong.

For a time, we would hold long online talks with these kids, trying to make them understand. But after a while, you start to spot the ones who have no interest in really listening. Some people will believe what they want to believe, no matter how much evidence you throw at them. If the legend sounds more interesting than reality, the legend often wins.

In July 2006, the police released more than 900 pages of evidence that had been seized from the Klebold and Harris homes, following years of court battles with the *Denver Post,* which had been suing for the release of the basement tapes.

Two crucial pieces of writing in particular were revealed. One of them was Dylan's diary, which had been mentioned in the original sheriff's report of 2000 but never actually seen. While Eric's inner feelings were on display for all to see thanks to his website, this was the first real look we got at what was in Dylan's mind.

Unlike Eric's writings, which were full of anger and threats, Dylan's diary paints a picture of a shy, lonely and self-loathing kid who wrote love letters and doubted that anyone would ever understand him. He wrote at length about the "zombies" of the world, stating, "The meek are trampled, the assholes prevail, the gods are deceiving, lost in my little insane asylum . . . I have lost my emotions, like in 'Hurt,' the song, NIN (Nine Inch Nails). People eventually find happiness. I never will. Does that make me a non-human? Yes, the god of sadness. . . ."

Dylan wrote at length about a girl he admired from afar as his "soulmate," though he indicated that she didn't return his feelings. "Unfortunately, even if you did like me the slightest bit, you would hate me if you knew who I was," he wrote.

Another entry featured "I love you" in big letters, and multiple drawings of hearts. Beside them Dylan wrote, "I hate this non-thinking stasis. I'm stuck in humanity. Maybe going NBK with Eric is the way to break free."

It's a striking contrast from the self-righteous venom that poured forth from Eric's keyboard. It also backs up what we'd been arguing based on Brooks's own experiences with Dylan: that he was likely following Eric's lead, seeking his friend's acceptance and approval, in planning the assault.

Also among the released evidence was a notepad owned by Eric's father, Wayne Harris. Wayne apparently began the journal shortly after the windshield incident. With the Harrises' continuing media silence, the notepad is the first glimpse we've gotten of Eric's family was dealing with his growing problems. Wayne took notes from his conversations with his son, Eric's denials of wrongdoing, his apologies, and phone numbers for getting him into the diversion program or seeking professional help.

However, the notebook also shows Wayne making excuses for his son. In regard to the windshield incident and the vandalism of Nick Baumgart's house, Wayne wrote, "We feel victimized, too. Brooks Brown is out to get Eric." He later added, "We don't want to be accused every time something supposedly happens. Eric is not at fault. . . . Brooks has problems (with) other boys. Manipulative + con artist."

Wayne was right about being manipulated. He just didn't realize which kid was the true con artist.

This latest batch of evidence continued to shed light on the case. However, even with the court's permission to release the basement tapes at last, new Jefferson County Sheriff Ted Mink chose not to do so, citing concerns about copycat incidents. With no challenges to that decision looming, it looks like this may be the final word. It could be that, at last, the public has all the Columbine information it will ever be allowed to see.

Time will tell how complete a picture we can get from it.

Both of us have made an effort in recent years to move on from Columbine. Like regular guys our age, we still get together for gaming sessions of *Guitar Hero* on Playstation 2 or marathons of *South Park*. We collaborated on a movie project, and we're both heavily involved in our own individual writing and video editing work. Columbine will never be forgotten, but after seven years it isn't healthy to dwell on it, either. It's important to find a balance.

Instead, we let *No Easy Answers* speak for us. We've received letters from as far away as Belgium and Australia, seen the book translated into

Japanese and watched as it continues to find an audience years after its release. It means a lot to know people still care after all this time. There are no easy answers. But we should never stop asking the questions.

Much has been learned from the story of Eric Harris and Dylan Klebold. But those lessons can be just as quickly forgotten.

We won't forget. Nor will we ever lose hope.

—Brooks Brown and Rob Merritt, July 2006